Early Interventions in Reading

Level K

Staff Development Guide

 SRA

Bothell, WA • Chicago, IL • Columbus, OH • New York, NY

Photo Credits

4 (tl) G.K. & Vikki Hart/Getty Images, (tr) Brand X Pictures/PunchStock, (bl) CORBIS, (br) Ingram Publishing/SuperStock; **23** (tr) Creatas/PunchStock, (tr) Tinke Hamming/Ingram Publishing, (bl) Bloomimage/CORBIS, (br) Stockbyte/PictureQuest; **37** (tl) Creative Crop/Getty Images, (tc) Comstock Images/Jupiter Images, (tr) Image Source/PunchStock, (bl) Darren Greenwood/Design Pics/CORBIS, (bc) Eyebyte/Alamy, (br) Brand X Pictures/PunchStock; **125** (t) Burke/Triolo Productions/Getty Images, (b) Image Source/PunchStock; **126** John A. Rizzo/Photodisc/Getty Images, **127** (r) Ingram Publishing/Alamy, (l) Comstock Images/Alamy.

MHEonline.com

Send all inquiries to:
McGraw-Hill Education
4400 Easton Commons
Columbus, OH 43219

ISBN: 978-0-02-114666-6
MHID: 0-02-114666-7

Printed in the United States of America.

6 7 8 9 QVS 19 18 17 16

The *McGraw-Hill* Companies

Table of Contents

Overview

Purpose

The purpose of *SRA Early Interventions in Reading,* Level K is to provide intensive small-group instruction in order to develop oral language, concepts of print knowledge, phonological and phonemic awareness, letter-sound correspondence knowledge, sight-word reading ability, and listening comprehension skills in emerging readers. A Quick Start Guide describing the first two lessons can be found later in this guide, on page 26.

SRA Early Interventions in Reading, Level K is a comprehensive emergent reading intervention for students at risk for developing reading problems or students with disabilities. It teaches multiple components of early reading in a series of engaging, fast-paced activities. The activities specifically designed to address the unique needs of English-language learners engage English-language learners in conversations about directions, vocabulary, the story selection, and other important concepts. Throughout the curriculum, skills and strategies are integrated over time, resulting in a set of lesson plans with overlapping content strands and extensive cumulative review and practice. The lessons target big ideas and provide extensive practice of key concepts and strategies. A hallmark of Level K is the integration of oral language and early alphabetic skills. This is designed to explicitly teach students how sounds and words relate to the meaning of text. Lessons include activities designed to do the following: teach concepts of print, promote phonological awareness, develop oral language, develop a deep understanding of the alphabetic principle and letter-sound correspondences, teach students how to segment and blend spoken words, provide practice sounding out decodable words composed of previously taught letter-sound correspondences, and use simple strategies to improve listening comprehension. The highly detailed lessons make instruction explicit, while allowing the teacher to respond to individual student learning needs.

Targeted Participants

SRA Early Interventions in Reading, Level K was specifically designed to develop oral language and emergent literacy and is appropriate for preschool students, kindergarten students who are English-language learners, kindergarten students who are at risk for becoming struggling readers or for developing a learning disability, and students in various grades with disabilities, such as intellectual disabilities (i.e., mental retardation). **Level K** provides extensive practice of the prerequisite skills that will prepare students for **Level 1** and provides extensive opportunities for oral-language development. In fact, the last lessons in **Level K** overlap concepts taught in **Level 1.** See further discussion later in this guide in the section called Placing Students in *SRA Early Interventions in Reading,* as well as the **Placement and Assessment Guide,** for more information about how to identify students who would benefit from instruction in **Level K** and how to place them in the appropriate lessons within the curriculum. For first-grade students who need additional oral-language support, the Read-Aloud lessons in **Level K** could be used in conjunction with **Level 1.**

Use of Instructional Time

SRA Early Interventions in Reading maximizes academic engagement by moving lessons along in a rapid manner with constant interchange between teacher and students. "Teacher talk" is kept to a minimum, and the phrases in teaching routines are used repeatedly in order to maximize time for student learning and to reduce student confusion. In a typical routine, you ask all students to respond in unison and then give individual turns that allow each student to demonstrate ownership of the content. Having students answer questions in unison ensures that each student practices all content rather than watching and listening as a peer responds. Most activities are done quickly and switch often to increase student engagement and motivation. However, during Read-Aloud activities and Language and Literacy support, answers to many questions will vary; therefore, it is important to give adequate think time and individual students opportunities to respond. Lessons are designed so that every two lessons relate to each other. The first lesson in each lesson pair includes a Read-Aloud activity and an activity that focuses on concepts of print. The Read-Aloud activity is designed to engage the students in discussions about texts in addition to the use of cues to signal unison student responses, as is done in most of the other activities. The second lesson in the lesson pair includes activities related to phonological and print awareness and links those to the selection that was read aloud in the previous lesson. A typical lesson includes either a Read-Aloud experience or three to six short activities that encompass multiple strands of content, such as phonemic awareness, letter naming, alphabetic decoding and encoding, and comprehension strategies.

The lessons generally require approximately 15–20 minutes to complete. However, the length of the lessons will vary according to student needs. English-language learners and students at risk for learning disabilities will typically be able to complete lessons more quickly than students with intellectual disabilities. Preschool students may complete fewer activities in a session than older students, due to a shorter attention span and less familiarity with structured small-group instruction. Sessions for preschool students may need to be only 5–10 minutes in length, so one lesson may require two sessions to complete. Smaller groups are particularly important for preschool students and students requiring more assistance with oral language. Smaller groups allow more opportunities to talk and develop oral language. Also, the time dedicated to each activity varies according to the nature of the content. Yet, reading activities requiring the most time are completed in less than ten minutes, except for the Read-Aloud lessons. There may be times when students struggle to master an activity in a lesson and the lesson takes too long. See the section in this guide on Mastery (page 16) for recommendations about what to do in those situations. For most students, the lessons are typically completed at a fast pace and the activities change every few minutes. A student with a short attention span is better able to stay focused on the task at hand when activities change frequently. Also, having quick, engaging activities is particularly beneficial for students at risk for learning disabilities, students with intellectual disabilities, English-language learners, and preschool students.

Presentation Techniques

SRA Early Interventions in Reading helps achieve superior outcomes through the various presentation techniques for delivering instruction. For example, the small-group design for instruction, with the students sitting in a semicircle around the teacher, allows the teacher to more readily give directions, offer think time, and elicit student responses. Another presentation technique is maintaining a fast pace throughout the lesson, moving quickly as students within the group are able to progress. The objective is to keep students focused and engaged while providing daily opportunities for them to develop greater ability in all aspects of reading and learning, including oral language, phonological and phonemic awareness, and letter-sound correspondence knowledge. The pacing is slower, however, during Read-Aloud activities. During Read-Aloud activities, students need time to talk about the selection, explore and use new vocabulary, and apply basic comprehension strategies. Although these activities do need to be sufficiently engaging and lively, they also need to allow students time to respond thoughtfully.

Most activities include opportunities for students to respond in unison, followed by individual practice. Clear and consistent visual and auditory cues are established to elicit responses from students in order to minimize teacher talk and maximize time spent learning for the students. Cue for group and individual responses throughout the lesson, consistently monitoring student responses and providing praise for correct responses and immediate corrective feedback for errors. It is important to try to maintain a ratio of four praise points for every one correction. Teachers must make on-the-spot judgments about why errors occur and must focus on that aspect of the task when providing corrective feedback.

The goal is to create a classroom based on positive feedback and support for students. Scaffolding during Read-Aloud activities should include modeling spoken sentences, often expanding on what a student says. Examples are provided later in this guide.

To enhance students' enthusiasm for learning, provide immediate and positive feedback for each activity as students complete activities, make progress, and demonstrate mastery. The Lesson Mastery Sheet lists each activity within each lesson. Mark each activity as it is completed so students will be able to see their accomplishments. When all students complete the activity with 100 percent accuracy on every item, place a check mark on the Lesson Mastery Sheet. If the students were not 100 percent accurate but demonstrated clear progress toward mastery, write a *P* for *Progress* on the Mastery Sheet instead of a check mark. See the Lesson Mastery Sheet section in this guide (page 17) for details about how to determine mastery, how to know when to continue in the curriculum or repeat a lesson, and what tools are available for monitoring student progress. You may also use the online tool to record mastery and progress on the Lesson Mastery Sheet.

Introduction to the Curriculum

Curriculum Strands and Objectives

As an integrated curriculum, the program provides a comprehensive framework for teaching students to read. Rather than being taught in isolation, one skill at a time, multiple strands are taught on a daily basis, and each strand is interrelated with the next. This design adds an element of relevancy that increases the effectiveness of the instruction. Students are not simply taught separate skills; rather they are taught how to apply skills learned in one activity (e.g., phonemic awareness blending) to new skills (e.g., sounding out words during the Stop-and-Go Game). Each strand is listed below with a brief explanation, the specific objective(s) for the strand, and a list of activities that address that strand. A more detailed explanation of the strands and activities is provided later in this guide.

Strand One: Oral Language and Vocabulary Development

This strand addresses language skills, including expressing thoughts, understanding directions, and engaging in discussions. Opportunities are provided to learn new, meaningful vocabulary that is connected to pictures used in the lessons or a **Read-Aloud** selection.

Objective:
- Students will develop oral-language skills by participating in discussions and reviewing vocabulary and concepts related to instructions and lessons.

Activities:
- Language and Literacy Support
- Read-Aloud
- Picture Naming

Strand Two: Listening Comprehension Strategies

Basic comprehension strategies are used to foster comprehension of stories read aloud.

Objective:
- Students will use a variety of very basic reading strategies, such as questioning, making predictions, and retelling, to comprehend text read orally.

Activity:
- Read-Aloud

Strand Three: Phonological Awareness

Phonological awareness activities help students develop an awareness that oral language consists of words and that words consist of sounds. These activities help students recognize words in sentences and sounds in words.

Objective:
- Students will recognize that sentences are composed of individual words, that words are composed of syllables, and that words rhyme if they have the same ending sounds.

Activities:
- Say and Move
- Syllable Clapping
- Rhyme Time

Strand Four: Phonemic Awareness

Phonemic awareness activities help students develop an awareness of the phonemes that make up spoken words. Practice with both stretching words (segmenting words) and blending words fosters phonemic awareness.

Objective:
- Students will say the first sound of a spoken word, blend phonemes to say words, and segment spoken words into sounds.

Activities:
- Stretching (segmenting)
  - First-Sound Pictures
  - First-Sound Game
  - Stretch-the-Word Game
  - Stop and Go
- Oral Blending
  - Say-the-Word Game
  - Stop and Go

Strand Five: Letter Names

Students are directly taught the names of all of the letters of the alphabet, and they practice identifying and writing the letters.

Objective:
- Students will associate names with letters.

Activities:
- Letter Names
- Writing the Letter

Strand Six: Concepts of Print

It is important for students to learn that there is a one-to-one correspondence between spoken words and groups of letters separated by spaces in a sentence. Students are explicitly taught through modeling how to recognize word placement in a sentence, relating spoken language to print.

Objective:
- Students will recognize word placement in sentences.

Activity:
- Point and Read

Strand Seven: Letter-Sound Correspondences

The most common letter-sounds for twelve letters are taught and extensively reviewed in Level K. (Remaining letter-sounds are taught in Level 1.) Students demonstrate mastery of each new letter-sound

correspondence before another letter-sound correspondence is introduced.

Objective:
- Students will associate sounds with letters.

Activities:
- Letter-Sound Introduction
- Letter-Sound Review

Strand Eight: Word Recognition

Students are taught high-frequency words that cannot be decoded phonetically with the letter-sounds they know. These are referred to as "tricky words."

Objective:
- Students will automatically recognize irregular words.

Activity:
- Tricky Words

Student Benefits

Beginning readers need a solid foundation of emergent literacy skills in order to become good readers. Level K of *SRA Early Interventions in Reading* provides carefully designed and integrated instruction and incorporates practice in critical emergent literacy skills to prepare students for Level 1 and/or core instruction. Instruction includes vocabulary, concepts of print, phonological and phonemic awareness, letter names, letter-sound correspondences, word recognition, and listening comprehension strategies. Throughout the activities, there is an emphasis on oral-language development, and there are many opportunities for students to use oral language when engaging in discussions, responding to texts, and exploring vocabulary. These would benefit students who are English-language learners or students with language development deficits, including students with disabilities such as intellectual disabilities or developmental disabilities.

All activities are designed to promote success for struggling readers, students at risk for learning disabilities, students with intellectual disabilities, English-language learners, and preschool students. *SRA Early Interventions in Reading,* Level K is highly motivational. Instruction and error techniques are designed to enable success and motivate all students to become better readers. Systematic review of previously learned material is provided in every lesson in order to promote mastery.

Without effective and early instruction of beginning literacy skills, students who lack emergent literacy knowledge will struggle to read. Level K of the *SRA Early Interventions in Reading* curriculum provides the critical content and clear instruction needed to equip emergent readers to become successful readers.

Motivation

SRA Early Interventions in Reading is designed to ensure few student errors and to provide every student with the best opportunity to succeed. Lessons are structured so that students go through a constant cycle of instruction, application, and review. The teacher models each skill before requiring students to perform that skill. After the teacher models, students usually perform the activities first in unison and then individually, until each student demonstrates ownership of the skill. In this way, students make few errors and feel competent.

Working toward mastery builds a sense of confidence and success in students. Getting the answer right is very reinforcing because students feel very smart! Consistently achieving mastery develops intrinsic motivation, instilling the desire within students to learn and achieve. Students are motivated to learn new material because

they know they will soon be given the opportunity to apply what they have learned to another activity, thus demonstrating their mastery. The opportunity to successfully apply newly learned material is rewarding to students.

With *SRA Early Interventions in Reading,* praise and tangible rewards provide additional sources of motivation for students. Praise should be genuine and frequent and should be given immediately after the response being recognized. Praise should be specific and relevant to the task at hand, offering useful information to the student; for example, "I like the way you sounded out that word, one sound at a time." Students then know what they did correctly and how they did it correctly so they can apply that information to the next task to achieve success again.

Tangible rewards include the use of check marks and stickers on the Lesson Mastery Sheet. It is important to give check marks and stickers only when students have achieved mastery or to write a *P* for *Progress* if students are making progress but have not achieved mastery. Students are very aware of this system and will work hard to earn the rewards.

The teacher's level of enthusiasm when presenting the materials is another primary source of motivation. This enthusiasm engages students from the very beginning and infuses them with a feeling of anticipation and excitement about what they will learn. You are encouraged to enjoy students' successes with them and let them know that you believe in them.

Each week students receive a Time to Shine Certificate to take home that relates information to families about what students have learned that week. This also allows the parents to get involved and share in their child's accomplishments, which provides additional motivation to succeed.

Intervention Basics

The instruction is designed for small groups of three to five students. A trained teacher meets with students for sessions of approximately 20 minutes a day, five days a week. The duration of the sessions can be shortened if necessary to meet students' needs. For example, preschool students may need to have 15-minute sessions, because they have shorter attention spans and have less stamina for structured instruction. It is possible that students who need a slower pace or more practice with an activity may not complete an entire lesson in one session. As the professional decision maker, the teacher determines the appropriate pacing so that students are paced through a lesson at the fastest rate at which they can achieve and maintain mastery, in order to keep motivation and engagement high. Since the lessons are cumulative and build on each other, it is essential that students reach mastery for each set of twenty lessons before moving on to the next set of twenty lessons.

Because students are receiving reading instruction in both the classroom and the intervention, they receive a double dose of reading. This approach creates an optimal situation for students to reach grade-level performance and to prevent future reading difficulties.

Materials

CURRICULUM MATERIALS
(Program-Provided)

- Teacher's Editions A, B, C
- Activity Book
- Read-Aloud Book
- Pictures for Language and Literacy Support
- Picture Magnets
- Letter-Sound Cards

- Placement and Assessment Guide (includes Lesson Mastery Sheets and Tricky Word Cards)
- Staff Development Guide
- Stop-and-Go Game
- Maxwell (puppet)
- Teaching Tutor (available online)

OTHER MATERIALS
(Teacher-Supplied)

- Magnetic marker board, marker, and eraser
- Easel

- Stickers
- Pencils

The list of curriculum materials helps to illustrate the variety of activities that contribute to making *SRA Early Interventions in Reading* a comprehensive curriculum. You will need the second list of materials in addition to those provided by the *SRA Early Interventions in Reading* curriculum. These materials guide you in providing the instruction struggling readers need in order to grow in ability, to stay on task, and to become skilled readers.

SRA Early Interventions in Reading, Level K: An Integrated Curriculum

The **SRA Early Interventions in Reading,** Level K curriculum is designed so that multiple strands are incorporated into all lessons: vocabulary and language development, listening comprehension strategies, phonological awareness, phonemic awareness, letter naming, letter-sound correspondences, and word recognition. Although strands are presented separately in this guide for clarity, each strand is interwoven with the others to create a cumulative effect. The parallel strands contain skills that are embedded in more advanced skills, until each student has mastered the strand. Over the course of the intervention, as the strands are mastered, students are on track to perform at grade level and are ready to learn the skills taught in Level 1.

Characteristics of Daily Lessons

Instruction is sequenced, and all elements are integrated. Each lesson consists of multiple strands and the skills used to teach those strands. The amount of new information introduced in any one lesson is kept to a minimum to help students as they assimilate only the immediate information. Most of each lesson is review and practice.

Classroom Arrangement

Each student needs to clearly see the **Teacher's Edition** and your cues during instruction, and students should sit close enough to you to hear all instructions. Students will also need an adequate amount of space at the table to complete writing tasks in the **Activity Book.**

You should sit so that all students can be seen clearly and so students' responses can be heard clearly. All students need to be monitored constantly, and they should be seated close enough to you that you can assist them during writing activities. Throughout the lessons there are activities in which you will need to turn quickly to the side and write on the marker board or use picture magnets on the board. When you use the marker board, it needs to be within easy reaching distance from your seat so you can maintain your instructional pace. A medium-sized magnetic marker board on an easel sitting to your side works very well for this.

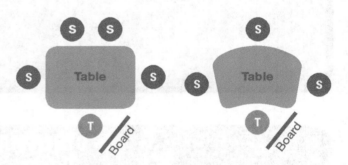

Students sit in a semicircle facing the teacher.

Scope and Sequence

A scope and sequence chart can be found in the appendix of each **Teacher's Edition.** This chart allows you to see at a glance which instructional strands are being taught in a given lesson and the skills being taught for the strands. To practice reading the scope and sequence chart, locate the first lesson in the chart. Run your finger across the row following the numeral 1 to see which specific skills are taught in the first lesson. To identify the strand for each skill, look for the strand name at the top of the column. For example, answering literal questions is a skill that is used to teach comprehension in the first lesson.

SRA Early Interventions in
Reading
Level K

SCOPE AND SEQUENCE

Lesson	Vocabulary Language Development	Phonological Awareness	Phonemic Awareness	Letter-Sound Correspondences	Letter Names	Word Recognition and Spelling		Reading	Comprehension Strategies
						Word Types	Tricky Words		
1								• Who Is in the Classroom?	• Comprehend text read orally • Answer literal questions about the text
2	• turn • sound • Say the names of objects represented by pictures		• Say the first sound of a spoken word that begins with a continuous sound	• Beginning Sound (continuous)	• T				
3	• cue	• Segment sentences into words						• Who Is in the Classroom?	
4	• stretch • trace		• Blend onsets (continuous) and rimes		• t				
5	• thermometer • healthy • safe • learn							• Who Helps Us?	
6									
7								• Who Helps Us?	
8					• Oo				
9	• bug • march • surprised • rest							• Insect Picnic	

Appendix 1 Scope and Sequence

Fully Specified Lessons

The lesson dialogues in the **Teacher's Editions** act as a guide for the teacher. They are prescriptive and highly detailed, and they spell out every aspect of each activity. Each lesson is designed to communicate only what the students need to learn that particular day. Teaching formats are presented in clear and consistent language, and they have been thoroughly tested to ensure success.

As you make instructional decisions regarding the lessons, such as when to provide more instruction, when to provide corrective feedback, and when to move on to the next activity, it is important to consider the needs of your students. Be sure to follow the format in order to maintain the fidelity of the intervention, but also be flexible and willing to adapt when needed in order to make sure your students are experiencing maximum success and growth. You have the freedom to address learning opportunities as they arise, even if these are not mentioned in the dialogues. Lessons should be reviewed prior to teaching them so they can be taught comfortably and quickly.

Routines

Using consistent formats reduces student confusion and enhances student learning. Using formats minimizes the amount of time students spend processing directions and maximizes the amount of time they practice skills. The formats are specific to the different strands. As students master skills, the formats evolve over time to accommodate students' continual progression toward becoming successful readers. Even routines that are familiar to the teacher should be reviewed briefly before the lesson is taught. By planning each lesson ahead of time, instruction is consistently clear, and guesswork on the part of the students is reduced.

The overarching teaching routine repeated throughout the curriculum is composed of the following steps: modeling new content, providing guided practice, and implementing individual practice in every activity. Preview and prepare for each lesson before its presentation to be clear about what is expected of both you and students in each activity. Teachers should be flexible during the Read-Aloud activity in order to capitalize on student interest and provide students with opportunities to talk about selections, use vocabulary words, and gradually increase their ability to express their own ideas in sentences. Students who speak in very short or incomplete sentences should gradually (i.e., across many lessons) increase the length and complexity of their spoken language during discussions. Teachers should model longer sentences that express the ideas of the student, not simply the ideas that are noted in the script.

Format Presentation

The lesson dialogues include what you say, what the correct student response is, and how you should respond based on the accuracy of the responses. Present lessons in a natural way, without necessarily reading the dialogue word by word. You may slightly alter the wording, as long as you maintain the integrity of the activity and preserve the intended goal of each activity. If students are responding correctly, then you can be assured that the wording you are using is effective. As much as you can, try to maintain eye contact with your students throughout the lesson presentation.

A sample activity is displayed below. As you review the sample activity, you will see that the **Teacher's Editions** use three different typefaces so you can easily recognize each part of the activity at a glance:

Bold blue type indicates what you say.

Bold red type indicates what the students say.

(Italic blue type in parentheses indicates what you do.)

Look at the sample activity.

Staff Development Guide, Level K

Look for dialogue that is written in bold blue type: **Now it's time to point and read.** This is what you say to your students.

Look for dialogue that is written in bold red type: **First, the rain whispers.** This is the correct answer that you want to hear from your students. If you don't get the correct answer, then you will need to provide an error correction. Specific error corrections are discussed later in this guide.

Look for dialogue that is written in blue and italics: *(Point to each word, moving your finger along the arrow.)* This is what you do. Any necessary cues appear in blue and italics also. You may be asked to model a skill for the students. These directions will vary from activity to activity, but they will be written in italic type also so that you will know at a glance what you are supposed to do.

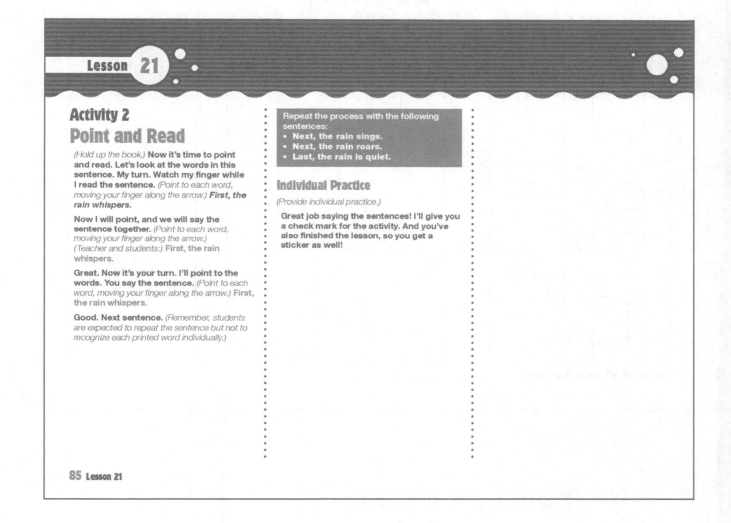

Lesson 21

Activity 2
Point and Read

(Hold up the book.) **Now it's time to point and read. Let's look at the words in this sentence. My turn. Watch my finger while I read the sentence.** *(Point to each word, moving your finger along the arrow.)* **First, the rain whispers.**

Now I will point, and we will say the sentence together. *(Point to each word, moving your finger along the arrow.)* *(Teacher and students:)* First, the rain whispers.

Great. Now it's your turn. I'll point to the words. You say the sentence. *(Point to each word, moving your finger along the arrow.)* First, the rain whispers.

Good. Next sentence. *(Remember, students are expected to repeat the sentence but not to recognize each printed word individually.)*

Repeat the process with the following sentences:
- **Next, the rain sings.**
- **Next, the rain roars.**
- **Last, the rain is quiet.**

Individual Practice

(Provide individual practice.)

Great job saying the sentences! I'll give you a check mark for the activity. And you've also finished the lesson, so you get a sticker as well!

85 **Lesson 21**

Activity Tracking Chart

An activity tracking chart is located in the appendix of each **Teacher's Edition.** This chart allows you to see where each specific skill or concept is introduced and taught within the curriculum. For instance, as shown in the chart below, in Lessons 1–10 the letters *t, o,* and *m* are introduced and reviewed.

SRA Early Interventions in Reading

ACTIVITY TRACK: Teacher's Edition A, Lessons 1–40

Lesson	ELD Activities	Picture Naming	First-Sound Pictures	Phonological Awareness (Say and Move)	Phonological Awareness (Multisyllabic Words)	Phonological Awareness (Complete Sentences)	Concepts of Print (Point and Read)	Writing the Letter	Rhyme Time	Letter (New/Review)	Sound Discrimination/Position	Oral Blending	Reading	Comprehension
1													• Who Is in the Classroom?	• Answer Literal Questions about the Text
2	• Taking turns • First sounds • Tracing	★	★					★		• T				
3	• Cues			★									• Who Is in the Classroom?	• Answer Literal Questions about the Text
4	• First sounds • Stretching • Tracing	★	★					★		• t • Review		★		
5	• Vocabulary: thermometer healthy safe learn			★									• Who Helps Us?	• Answer Literal Questions about the Text
6		★	★					★		• Review		★		
7	• Vocabulary review			★									• Who Helps Us?	• Answer Literal Questions about the Text
8		★	★					★		• Oo • Review		★		
9	• Vocabulary: bug march surprised rest			★									• Insect Picnic	• Answer Literal Questions about the Text
10		★	★					★		• M • Review	• Beginning Sound	★		

Appendix 10 Activity Track Chart

Critical Features of Lesson Delivery

There are three critical features for successful implementation of the materials: pacing, error correction, and teaching to mastery. All three must be present to achieve the level of success possible with the program. A well-paced lesson promotes motivation, engagement, and concept retention. Students are provided every minute of instruction with many opportunities to respond, ensuring that each student gets enough practice with concepts and skills to gain ownership of the practiced content.

Pacing

Instructional Pacing

Instructional pacing is a critical factor in the presentation of these lessons and can make or break the effectiveness of instruction. The objective is to go as fast as the students can go, without going faster than they can handle. In other words, students need just enough "think time" to respond to items correctly. More think time is needed for more complex questions regarding vocabulary and listening comprehension. Less think time is needed for skills that should become automatic, such as letter naming and letter-sound correspondence.

More think time is needed when skills are first introduced and less when they are nearly mastered. In a well-paced lesson the dialogue between you and the students occurs as a rapid interchange. Even discussion during Read-Aloud should move fairly quickly, yet allow students time to express their ideas. Individual responses typically should be only a sentence or two. Fast pacing greatly increases academic engagement because students pay closer attention to the material being presented. Fast pacing also increases learning by reducing behavior problems and keeping students involved and on task.

Pacing should be fast enough to keep students attending and on task, but not so fast that they begin to guess and make errors. Pacing should be rapid. When students respond correctly, move quickly to the next instance or task. There should be minimal extraneous language—from you or the students—or off-task behavior during transitions. With good pacing, you will be able to elicit about ten responses per minute from each student during basic routines such as letter-sound correspondence. If the pacing is appropriate, students receive more practice time and have an increased opportunity for achieving success.

Ensuring Academic Reponses with Cues

To achieve good pacing, you use a variety of cues. A cue indicates when students answer and enables students to respond in unison, increasing the amount of practice time. Cues used to elicit student responses are either visual or auditory, depending on the activity.

- Visual cues are used when the students are looking at you or at the **Teacher's Edition.**
- Auditory cues are used when the students are working from the **Activity Book.**

Using cues helps you control pacing and provide appropriate think time for students before they answer. The use of cues minimizes students' tendency to guess or blurt out incorrect answers when they do not take time to think before answering.

The basic routine of each activity includes unison responses followed by individual practice. Students feel safer when answering in unison. Unison responses provide maximum opportunity for students to practice each skill as it is being taught. Cueing is an effective technique for keeping students together, maintaining a lively pace, and increasing automaticity of response.

Most students, even preschool students or students with disabilities, can be taught to respond in unison. However, occasionally students with significant needs may not be able to respond in unison. In these unusual cases, students should respond individually until unison responses are achieved.

Different formats require different cues. Be consistent to help students learn which cue is associated with each of the skills. Clarity of cues is essential to ensure that you move smoothly through tasks during instructional time. You will quickly find the cues that work best with your teaching style. The key is to be consistent with the cues and to keep them crisp and quick so that students know exactly when they are expected to respond. Some groups of students will require more practice than others to learn to respond in unison.

TYPES OF CUES

STRAND	RECOMMENDED CUE
All Strands	**Hand Drop:** Cue is used to ensure that students will think before they provide an answer to a question. It can be used to elicit individual or unison responses. **Implementation of cue:** As you ask a question, hold your hand at your shoulder level with your palm facing outward. Give approximately two seconds of think time, and then drop your hand with a slashing motion indicating that you are ready for the students' answer.
Vocabulary	**Touch:** Cue enables students to use vocabulary to identify objects in pictures. **Implementation of cue:** Hold the marker board with one hand so all students can see the picture magnets (or use a large marker board on an easel). Touch under each picture, cueing students to say the name of the picture.
Phonemic Awareness First Sound	**First Sound:** Cue enables students to identify the first sound they hear within a word. **Implementation of cue:** Hold your right fist at shoulder level so the back of your hand is facing the students. Raise your index finger, cueing students to say the sound while reinforcing left-to-right directionality.
Phonemic Awareness Stretching and Blending	**Stretching Words:** Cue enables students to identify each sound they hear within a word. **Implementation of cue:** Hold your right fist at shoulder level so the back of your hand is facing the students, and hold up one finger for each sound within a word.
Point and Read	**Think and Say:** Cue guides students as they echo-read a sentence. **Implementation of cue:** Point to the dot at the beginning of each word to draw students' attention to the word. Pause briefly, and then glide your finger across the arrow as the students say the word.
Letter Names and Word Recognition	**Touch:** Cue guides students as they say letter names or tricky words. **Implementation of cue:** Hold the **Teacher's Edition** so all students can see the letters/words. Touch under each letter/word, cueing students to say the name of the letter/word.
Letter-Sound Correspondences	**Point-Touch:** Cue guides students as they say each sound in a letter-sound review activity. **Implementation of cue:** Point to the letter-sound, pause, and touch under the letter-sound for students to read. Students say the sound as you touch under each letter-sound. Students hold the sound for as long as you touch under the letter or letter combination. Hold your finger under the letter-sound for two or three seconds for continuous sounds; touch quickly under stop sounds.

Small-Group Rules

You will establish four rules from the very beginning to prepare students to observe and to respond properly to cueing:

1. Sit tall.
2. Listen big.
3. Answer when I cue.
4. Answer together.

A quick reminder is inserted in lesson presentation dialogues periodically. Provide additional reminders to students as often as needed. You may add additional rules at your own discretion. These might include: Eyes up front. Watch me.

Error Corrections

It is important to give immediate corrective feedback to your students when they make an error. This means all errors are corrected as soon as they occur. When an error occurs, model the fact by telling the fact: **My turn.** When you model, you literally do the task for the students, telling them the correct response. Next, you ask *all* the students to repeat the item with you: **Do it with me.** Then, have students say the correct response without you: **Your turn.** In this way, you do not single out the student who made the error and you ensure that all students are maintaining attention. When the teacher corrects errors immediately and provides opportunities to practice the task again, students can become more successful. Errors should also be corrected during oral language and listening comprehension activities. In these cases the teacher should model appropriate language. The length of the sentences modeled by the teacher should be determined by the students. If the students are unable to repeat a sentence, the teacher should shorten the sentence. If students answer in very short sentences or phrases, the teacher should model a slightly longer sentence and have the students repeat the slightly longer sentence. When providing individual turns,

it is not essential that the child repeat a sentence verbatim as long as the child's sentence represents the correct meaning and a gradual improvement in that child's spoken language. In other words, the goal is for students to gradually learn to express their ideas in longer, more complex sentences.

ERROR CORRECTION TECHNIQUES

Model: My turn.
Lead: Do it with me.
Test: Your turn.

Mastery

The lessons are designed so that new skills are introduced only when students have been given extensive practice with previous skills. In any given lesson, the majority of the lesson is review, and a small portion is introduction or practice of new skills. Because every lesson has only a minimal amount of new information introduced, the goal is for student mastery of every activity in every lesson. Teaching to mastery ensures that students will be ready to move forward in the strand without the lessons becoming too difficult. Mastery communicates that what is learned today is important because it will be needed in later lessons.

A skill is considered mastered when every student is able to perform the skill independently without making any mistakes. The goal in each activity is to teach the skills to mastery before moving to the next activity. However, there may be a time when the students are having difficulty with a certain activity. In this instance, provide corrective feedback and continued practice until the students make progress toward mastery, meaning that they make fewer mistakes than when you first started the activity. You can then mark a *P* for *Progress* on the Lesson Mastery Sheet.

If, after corrective feedback and additional practice, students do not make progress and the lesson is taking too long, move on to the next activity, and come back to that activity later. This will typically occur more often with students with intellectual disabilities than with students at risk for learning disabilities or English-language learners. Also, preschool students may not be able to achieve mastery within one session because of shorter attention spans and less familiarity with structured small group instruction. Be flexible when teaching for mastery. Consider your students' needs, their attention spans, and how they are progressing. Avoid frustrating students or sticking with an activity so long that it discourages students and reduces motivation to learn. Determining mastery for vocabulary and oral language development activities, primarily those during Read-Aloud, is more challenging than determining mastery of basic skills such as letter-sounds. For these activities, use your judgment to determine if students understand the meanings of words and are answering questions accurately. Students should also make progress in their ability to express their ideas in phrases and sentences, gradually increasing the length and complexity of their oral language. For students with significant language needs, you may want to collaborate with a speech-language therapist to set goals for the length of sentences in the spoken language of your students.

Determining Mastery

Mastery is assessed and determined mostly during the independent practice portion of the activities. Each student in the group must demonstrate the skill during independent practice with no errors. If a student makes an error, use the appropriate correction procedure, and practice the specific skill repeatedly until the student has mastered it. If a student needs any assistance, mastery has not been achieved.

Some students, especially students at risk for learning disabilities, students with intellectual disabilities, English-language learners, and preschool students, might struggle to reach mastery with certain activities. As long as students are improving with the task, you can continue to the next activity and write a P on the Mastery Sheet for Progress. However, before going on to the next set of twenty lessons, it is important that all students have reached mastery with all the skills, because the next set of twenty lessons is more difficult. This is explained further in the following sections.

Individual Practice

It is during individual practice that you determine whether each student has truly mastered the activity or if you need to provide additional group practice. After group responses, call on each student individually to complete a few items or read a few sentences. Give each student one to three items during individual practice. You may need to give a stronger student only one item but a weaker student two or three items to ensure mastery. Typically you should call on lower-performing students first. Then you will call on a higher-performing student while encouraging the other students to just think of the answer and not say it aloud. When all students can complete the task independently and without error, you know the group has achieved 100 percent mastery. As a rule, if more than two errors occur during individual practice, the group needs more practice.

Lesson Mastery Sheet

At the end of each activity, tell students if they have mastered the skill or made progress with the skill being taught. When all students have completed the activity with 100 percent accuracy on every item, place a checkmark on the Lesson Mastery Sheet. If the students were not 100 percent accurate but demonstrated clear progress toward mastery, write a P for Progress on the Mastery Sheet instead of a checkmark.

Because certain activities are repeated within a set of twenty lessons, 100 percent mastery is not essential with those activities with every lesson. As long as students are making progress towards mastery, you can proceed to the next lesson. Writing a *P* for *Progress* on the Mastery Sheet instead of making a check will help you better keep track of progress and make instructional decisions as you proceed. It is important, however, that students have reached mastery by the end of each set of twenty lessons. Although a skill might be continued in the next set of lessons, the level of difficulty increases. Because the curriculum is designed to gradually and cumulatively become more complex, a large portion of each lesson is composed of review and generalization work; each lesson has a mixture of review and new material. Thus, if mastery has been achieved on previous lessons, students should easily achieve mastery on new lessons.

At the end of each set of twenty lessons, evaluate student progress using both the Mastery Sheet and the student assessments (discussed in the next section). If students continue to struggle with certain skills, provide review of those skills before going on to the next lessons.

Lesson Mastery Sheet

Teacher ____________ **Group** ____________

Students ____________ ____________

____________ ____________

____________ ____________

Lesson \ Activity	1	2	3	4	5	6	7	8	9	10	Mastery
1			★	★	★	★	★	★	★	★	
2						★	★	★	★	★	
3				★	★	★	★	★	★	★	
4							★	★	★	★	
5				★	★	★	★	★	★	★	
6							★	★	★	★	
7			★	★	★	★	★	★	★	★	
8						★	★	★	★	★	
9			★	★	★	★	★	★	★	★	
10							★	★	★	★	

Make one copy for each group of students.

Placement and Assessment Guide, Level K

10 Mastery Sheet

Measuring Mastery through Progress Monitoring

A series of student assessments is provided in the **Placement and Assessment Guide** for use in assessing student mastery of the skills presented in each set of twenty lessons. Students are assessed for mastery and generalization of picture naming, segmenting and blending phonemes, letter names, and letter-sound correspondences. An assessment is administered every twentieth lesson. The assessments are not timed.

These in-program assessments are a powerful tool for both monitoring student progress and evaluating your presentation of lesson content. Student performance on the assessments allows you to evaluate if students are learning what you are teaching, indicating if your lesson-presentation pacing is appropriate, and helping you determine when reteaching is necessary and when to move on without reteaching. Administering the student assessments is a valuable way to ensure that students are truly mastering lesson content and building the foundation for skills introduced in subsequent lessons.

As mentioned in the section on the Lesson Mastery Sheet, the student assessments are also valuable tools for ensuring that students who were previously making progress on skills have mastered those skills before moving on to the next set of lessons. This will ensure that students can build on the mastered skills from previous lessons with the new skills taught in the new lessons.

Placing Students in SRA Early Interventions in Reading

In order to appropriately place students in the *SRA Early Interventions in Reading* program, you should administer a reliable and valid screening measure during the first several weeks of the school year. Schools and classrooms routinely give such tests to all students at the beginning of the year. If such tests are not routine at your school, initial teacher observations can be helpful in spotting students who should be screened to determine if they would benefit from *SRA Early Interventions in Reading.*

One quick way to spot students in need of this intervention is to watch for students who are struggling to master letter-naming, letter-sounds, and phonemic awareness skills instruction provided during the first several weeks of the school year. Of course, it becomes easier to notice students who are not making progress as each week passes. However, it is important to identify students who need extra help as soon as possible, because every day that passes allows students to fall farther and farther behind their peers. Our goal for all students is grade-level reading skills by the end of the year; the farther behind children fall at any point of the year, the more difficult it is for them to achieve that goal.

Level K is also appropriate for typically developing preschool students, as these skills should be mastered by late preschool or kindergarten. If the program is used with typically developing preschool students, these students may benefit from a faster pace. In this case, consider reducing the amount of repetition, being careful that students are demonstrating mastery of skills.

Placing students in the appropriate lessons is an essential part of ensuring student success in *SRA Early Interventions in Reading.* Once a student has been identified as potentially benefiting from an early intervention curriculum, through either an outside test of skills or by teacher observations, consider which level of **SRA Early Interventions in Reading** would be most appropriate for your students. Kindergarten teachers should use Level K. Level K is appropriate for kindergarten students who need additional support. First-grade teachers should consider whether Level K or Level 1 is most appropriate for the individual students. Level 1 is appropriate for most first-grade students who need some additional instruction with beginning reading skills; however, Level K is appropriate for first-grade students who struggle with language or need slower-paced, more intensive instruction, such as students at high risk for learning disabilities, English-language learners, and students with intellectual disabilities. If Level K is used with first-grade students, care should be taken to move these students as quickly as possible through Level K. Because the content taught at the end of Level K overlaps with the beginning of Level 1, consider skipping either the last 20 lessons of Level K or the first 20 lessons of Level 1. For first-grade students in need of extensive oral language development, you may consider beginning in Level 1 and concurrently conducting the Read-Aloud activities from Level K.

After determining which level of **SRA Early Interventions in Reading** is most appropriate, administer the in-program Placement Test. The Placement Test consists of a series of short activities designed to mirror the content of the intervention materials at different points in the curriculum. Based on a student's demonstrated mastery of the skills in each of the Placement Test sections, either administer the next section of the test to the student, place the student in the designated lesson within the curriculum, or move the student out of the intervention group to receive instruction in only the primary reading materials.

Time to Shine

Each week, you will send home with students a Time to Shine Certificate. On this certificate, you will list the new letter names, letter-sound correspondences, vocabulary, and tricky words that the student has mastered throughout the week. The Time to Shine Certificate establishes and maintains a connection between the teacher and each student's parents or guardian. A blackline master version of the Time to Shine Certificate, in both English and Spanish, can be found in the **Placement and Assessment Guide.**

Reflective Teaching

Even though *SRA Early Interventions in Reading* is very structured, you will still need to reflect on your teaching to understand why your instruction is or is not having the desired effect with specific students. The purpose of this reflection is to gain awareness of your teaching practices and to formulate a plan of action to improve instruction as needed through critical decision-making. Tailoring instruction to meet the needs of individual students and groups of students is a critical part of the success of *SRA Early Interventions in Reading.* It may be helpful for you to keep a journal to document successes and challenges. (Journal entries should be made immediately after a lesson is finished and not during the actual lesson.) Over time, the journal entries will allow you to look for recurring patterns as you reflect on the needs of your students. It is also helpful to discuss both successes and challenges with colleagues, intervention coaches, or other educators. As you make decisions about how to adapt your instruction to meet the needs of your students, be careful to maintain the integrity of the instruction and preserve the intended goal of each activity. Always consider the objectives of a given activity or lesson to determine if your students are progressing toward accomplishing the objectives.

Teaching Special Populations

Reflective teaching and adapting the lessons are particularly important when teaching special populations of students, such as students at risk for developing learning disabilities, students with intellectual disabilities, English-language learners, and preschool students. Although the structure and pacing of the lessons are designed to benefit such learners, as the professional decision-maker, you use the curriculum as a tool to meet your students' needs. Use the curriculum flexibly and adapt it to include reteaching, additional scaffolding, or other modifications as necessary. The lessons and dialogue should be viewed as a resource and guide to ensure the fidelity of the curriculum, not as a strict, rigid script of what must be said and done every session. It is important to remember that you can adapt the lessons to respond to the needs of your students, while being sure to preserve the intended instructional goal and routine of each activity, thus helping students reach mastery with all the skills. Suggestions for possible adaptations are provided throughout the rest of this guide. Look for the *In the Real World* boxes for specific ideas.

The Phonology of English

While English has twenty-six letters in its alphabet, it is composed of many more than twenty-six speech sounds. Linguists estimate that English has between forty-two and forty-four different sounds, and this number may be slightly higher or lower depending on many variables, including regional and individual differences in speech and changes in how sounds are stressed. These individual speech sounds are called phonemes. A phoneme is the smallest unit of sound that can make a difference in meaning. The conventions for spelling the forty-four phonemes in English pose a very difficult task for many children and even for some adults. English sounds have hundreds of graphemes, or written representations of sounds. Take, for example, the five letters most commonly used to represent vowel sounds: *a, e, i, o, u.* These five letters are but the tip of the iceberg. There are actually eighteen vowel phonemes in English, and there are eighty ways they are commonly spelled (eighty common graphemes). Think about how these eighteen vowel phonemes sound. For example, consider all the differences in your lip and tongue positions when you say these words: *three, cake, ought, moon, hat, coil.* Notice that your lips are pursed, stretched, or open. Your tongue is either touching your teeth, between your teeth, just behind your teeth, or on the roof of your mouth. Consider the many different graphemes that helped spell those vowel sounds: $\overline{ee}$, *a_e, ough,* $\overline{oo}$, *a, oi.*

Consonant phonemes make up the other twenty-six sounds of English. In some ways, the spelling of consonant phonemes is less complicated than the spelling of vowel phonemes in English, because there is a one-to-one correspondence between the letter and the sound for eighteen of the consonant phonemes. In other words, the /d/ sound is spelled with a *d,* the /t/ sound is spelled with a *t,* and so on. There are seven consonant phonemes that are represented by two letters (for example, the /sh/ sound is spelled *sh;* the /ch/ sound is spelled *ch*). These are called digraphs because the two-letter spelling represents one phoneme. They are sometimes confused with consonant blends, which are simply two or more consonant phonemes side by side, with each retaining its original sound (the blend of /str/ is made up of three phonemes: /s/, /t/, and /r/). There are some consonants that do not have a unique phoneme assigned to them, including *c* and *x.* The letter *c* represents either the /k/ sound or the /s/ sound, and the letter *x* represents the /ks/ sound.

Finally, consonant phonemes are divided into voiced and unvoiced sounds. In voiced consonants, the vocal cords vibrate. For example, *zoo* sounds different from *Sue* because the *z* is voiced. In contrast, in unvoiced consonants, the vocal cords do not vibrate: *pit, fit.* Have students put their hands on their vocal cords to feel the vibration. Often, in the American dialect of English, unvoiced consonants like *t* that are sandwiched between two voiced vowels are "voiced": *biting* and *butter.* These are called "flaps," and many speakers of British English do not use this pronunciation.

Teaching and the Phonology of English

Up to this point, the discussion of the phonology of English has relied on some technical language, such as *phoneme, grapheme, digraph,* and *blend.* However, when teaching children, such formal language is *not* used. Students do not need to know the theoretical concepts, but they are instead encouraged to develop automaticity in recognizing different letter-sound combinations. As you teach the **SRA Early Interventions in Reading** curriculum, you will become increasingly familiar with the structure of English because the curriculum is carefully laid out to follow certain principles of English phonology. To help you develop some of this background knowledge—or to refresh you on what you might have learned already—below is a review of some of the major components and terms of the phonology of English that are particularly useful when teaching the **SRA Early Interventions in Reading** curriculum.

Continuous and Stop Sounds

Continuous sounds are sounds that can be held, hummed, or sung. The most obvious continuous sounds are vowels: all vowel sounds are continuous, including long and short vowels, *r*-controlled vowels, (vowels that change their sounds slightly when followed by *r*), diphthongs (a blend of vowels in one syllable, such as *oy* in *boy* and *ow* in *now*), and schwa (the vowel sound sometimes heard in an unstressed syllable). Continuous consonants include: *f, l, m, n, r, s, v, w, y, z*. When you are teaching the **SRA Early Interventions in Reading** curriculum, you will hold the continuous sounds for two to three seconds. Holding continuous sounds makes sounding out and reading words the fast way easier for students.

Stop sounds are sounds that block the passage of air as the sound is completed. You cannot hold the /t/ sound, for example, because the very act of making the sound stops the flow of air. The stop sounds are consonants: *b, c, d, g, h, j, k, p, q, t*. Say the stop sounds quickly without distorting the sound. For example, the /b/ sound should not be distorted by the sound /uh/ at the end of it.

Although continuous sounds and stop sounds are presented differently during instruction (continuous sounds are held for two to three seconds and stop sounds are spoken quickly), students do not have to learn the labels for each sound. Students need to be able to say the sounds correctly, holding continuous sounds and saying stop sounds quickly, but they do not need to label the sound. This is particularly

important when playing the Stop-and-Go Game. During the game, the teacher, not the student, labels the sounds as stop or go (i.e., continuous).

Syllable Types

A syllable is a unit of pronunciation that has one and only one vowel sound. There are six common syllable types in English spelling: closed, open, *r*-controlled, vowel team, silent *e*, and consonant *-le*. Students are never explicitly taught the labels for each of these; however, the curriculum is written with a clear understanding of these syllable types so students are exposed to them. The closed syllable type is the only syllable type taught in Level K. Other syllable types are taught in Level 1.

Closed: The vowel sound is usually short, and the single vowel is usually followed by a consonant *(cat, rabbit)*.

Open: A syllable ends with a single vowel sound, which is usually long *(me, tree)*.

r-controlled: The vowel in the syllable is followed by an r, which changes its sound so that the sound is not long or short *(heart, danger)*.

Vowel-team: Two or more letters can together make a single vowel sound in the syllable *(rain, head, spoil)*. Notice that these can be long, short, or diphthongs.

Silent e: A syllable with the vowel-consonant-silent e pattern *(make, rope)*.

Some terms, like long *e* and short *e*, which are probably familiar to you, are avoided in this curriculum. Instead, students are taught to develop automaticity and to recognize the sounds they see, not the labels that go with the rules.

The Sound Pronunciation Guide on the following pages corresponds to the sounds and spellings taught in **SRA Early Interventions in Reading.**

Sound Pronunciation Guide

/aaa/	lamb, am	/āāā/	age	/b/	ball, bat, cab
		_a	label, baby		
		_ai	bait, mail, aid		
		_ay	day, play, away		
		a_e	vane, lane		
		eigh	eight, weigh		
		ea	break, great		
/k/	camera	/d/	dinosaur, dad	/eee/	hen, red
c	cat, car			ea	head, bread
k	kitten, kite				
ck	pack, sack				
/ēēē/	eat	/fff/	fan	/g/	gopher, dog
_e	be, he	f	fish, if		
ee	seed, feed	ph	photo, phone		
ea	read, bead				
e_e	eve				
_y	very, happy				
_ie	families				
/h/	hound, hat	/iii/	pig, it	/īīī/	icy
				i	item, ivy
				_y	my, reply
				i_e	pine, ride
				_ie	tie, pie, flies
				_igh	right, light
/j/	jump	/lll/	lion	/mmm/	monkey
j	jar, major	l	lake, tall	m	man, yummy
ge	gentle, page	-le	bottle, apple	_mb	climb, limb
_dge	bridge, ridge				
gi	giant				
/nnn/	nose	/ooo/	frog, on	/ōōō/	open
n	not, sun			o	over, go
kn_	knot, knee			_ow	own, grow
				o_e	note, rode
				oa_	oak, toad
				_oe	toe, doe
/p/	popcorn, map	/qu/	quack, queen	/rrr/	robot
				r	run, red
				wr_	wrap, wrong

Sound Pronunciation Guide

/sss/ **s** **ce** **ci_**	sausage so, pass cent, face circle, city	**/t/**	timer, Tom, toast	**/u/**	tug, up
/ūūū/ **u** **_ew** **u_e** **_ue**	use unit, menu few, pew cube, fuse cue, fuel	**/vvv/**	vacuum, velvet	**/www/**	washer, wow
/ks/	exit, ax, fox	**/yyy/**	yaks, yes, yell	**/zzz/** **z** **_s**	zipper zoo, maze was, laws
/sh/	shark, ship, mash	**/arr/**	armadillo, car, jar	**/th/**	feather, that, them
/ch/ **ch** **_tch**	chipmunk cherry, church crutch, patch	**/err/** **er** **ir** **ur**	bird farmer, fern dirt, stir fur, burn	**/ing/**	king, sing
/th/	thimble, think, three	**/wh/**	whales, white	**/all/** **al** **all**	ball also, almost call, tall
/or/	corn, form, order	**/ol/**	cold, told, old	**-ed, pronounced** **/ed/** **/d/** **/t/**	 handed, glided filled, named hoped, roped
/ow/ **ow** **ou_**	cow down, howl loud, out	**/aw/** **aw** **au_**	hawk jaw, dawn caught, sauce	**/ōo/** **oo** **_ew** **_ue** **u_e** **o** **ui** **oe** **u**	goo too, roof blew, new blue, glue rule, tube do, who suit, fruit shoe, canoe tuna, ruby
/ŏo/ **oo** **u**	foot soot put, bush	**/oi/** **oi** **_oy**	coil boil, coin boy, toy	**ere** **eer** **ear**	here deer hear
_are	care, share				

Quick Start Guide

This section is provided as a way to quickly begin instruction with Lessons 1–2 of Level K. A summary of the activities included in the first two lessons is provided here. See the sample lesson pages provided after the guidelines for the dialogue and more specific instructions. After each activity is completed without errors, write a check mark on the Mastery Sheet for the activity. See the Mastery section in this guide for more information about how to know if students have mastered an activity and what to do when students struggle to demonstrate mastery.

Lesson 1

Activity 1: Rules

It is important to begin by explaining the four rules: Sit tall. Listen big. Answer when I cue. Answer together. State the rule, explain it, and have students practice it. You may add additional rules at your own discretion. These might include: Eyes up front. Watch me.

Activity 2: Read-Aloud

In this activity the teacher reads the selection aloud, engaging the student in discussion before, during, and after the selection is read. Although specific dialogue is provided, it is a guide and not a script that must be followed verbatim. Walk your students through the steps good readers take to read and comprehend text: preview the selection and vocabulary, read the selection and monitor comprehension, and respond to the selection after reading. Specifically for Lesson 1, preview the selection by reading the title. Have students read the title with you and then without you. Discuss who is actually in the classroom.

Provide opportunities for students to respond individually. Read the selection aloud. Then read it aloud again and have students answer the questions from the selection with you. After reading, practice saying the names in the selection. First, read the names. Then, have students read the names with you. Last, call on individual students to read the names. If desired, you may wish to create your own book, modeled after the selection, using pictures of your students and their names. This is particularly helpful for students with intellectual disabilities or extremely low language skills.

Lesson 2

Activity 1: Rules

Remind students of the rules: Sit tall. Listen big. Answer when I cue. Answer together. Remind students they need to follow the rules to become better readers.

Activity 2: Picture Naming

For English-language learners, begin the activity by teaching the word *turn,* and explain what it means to take turns.

For all students, show the **Teacher's Edition.** Point to each picture, say the name of the picture, and then have students say the name in unison. Then, quickly point to each picture, and have students say the names of the animals in unison. Last, provide individual practice naming the animals. This is an ideal time to practice answering in unison. If students do not answer in unison, have them repeat the item until they answer it in unison (i.e., with your signal).

Activity 3: First-Sound Pictures

For English-language learners, begin the activity by teaching what a *first sound* is, and give some examples of words and their first sounds.

For all students, tell your students they will be listening for the first sound in each word. Two pictures at a time, show pictures and tell students the names of the pictures, emphasizing the first sound by stretching it (you will notice that all of the words begin with continuous sounds that can be stretched). Then, say the first sound of one of the pictures, and ask students which picture begins with that sound. Continue the activity with additional sets of two pictures. Provide individual practice. Again, be careful to require unison responses. Simply repeat the cue until all students respond in unison. This repetition should be conducted playfully by saying phrases such as "Don't let me trick you." Presenting it to the students as a game and praising them for unison responses are important.

Activity 4: Letter Introduction

Use the *Tt* letter-sound card (but cover the lowercase *t* with a sticky note) to introduce the letter *T*. Point to the letter and tell students the letter name. Have students say the letter with you multiple times as you tap the card to cue their unison response. Show students the **Teacher's Edition.** Read *Tom Tuttle.* Point out the *T* in *Tom* and the *T* in *Tuttle.* Point to the *T* and have students say the name. Then, pass out **Activity Books** and pencils. Point to a *T* and say the name. Have students point to a *T* and say the name. Next, model circling a *T* and saying the name, and then have students circle each *T* and say the name as they circle it. Don't forget to praise students for unison responses.

Activity 5: Writing the Letter

For English-language learners, begin the activity by making sure students know what *dot* and *trace* mean. Draw, model, and discuss the terms as needed.

For all students, hold up the *Tt* letter-sound card with the lowercase *t* covered with a sticky note. Tell students they will learn how to write the letter *T.* Use your finger to make a *T* in the air and say, **down, across, T.** Then have students make a *T* in the air with you, while everyone says **down, across, T.** Pass out the **Activity Books** and pencils. Model how to write the letter *T,* saying **down, across, T** as you write. Have students trace and write the letter in their books as they softly say **down, across, T.**

MATERIALS

1. *Read-Aloud*, pages 1–5

OBJECTIVES

Activity 1 *Rules*
• Establish rules

Activity 2 *Comprehension Strategies*
• Comprehend text read orally
• Answer literal questions about the text

Activity 1
Rules

Students, my name is _____. I am going to be one of your reading teachers this year. Let's introduce ourselves. *(Take a few moments to learn each student's name and to let students greet each other.)*

Now that we know one another's names, we need to talk about a few things. We are going to be working together each day for reading. In order for you to become the very best readers, you have to learn some rules about how to behave when we work together.

(Explain and model each of the following rules. You may want to add other rules, such as "Eyes up front" or "Do your best.")

Sit tall.

Listen big. *(This means no talking while the teacher is talking.)*

(Have students demonstrate each rule. You might need to prompt them by saying something like "Show me sitting tall.")

When you work hard and follow these rules, you will become better readers. I expect you to follow these rules every day. If you follow these rules, we will finish our lessons, and you will become good readers.

(Discuss the merits of becoming a better reader. You might want to say "Tell me why it is important to be a good reader." Explain the mastery measurement system and how students earn check marks and stickers on the lesson Mastery Sheets. Remember to praise students for following the rules throughout the rest of the lesson. Put a check mark on the lesson Mastery Sheet for this activity.)

Lesson 1

Activity 2
Read-Aloud

Part A: Preview

(Hold up Read-Aloud page 1.) **I'm going to read something from this book to you. The name of the story I'm going to read is *Who Is in the Classroom?***

My turn to say the name. *(Point to the title.)* ***Who Is in the Classroom?***

Now let's say the name together. *(Call on a student.)*

(Teacher and student:) ***Who Is in the Classroom?***
Good. Your turn. Say the name. Who Is in the Classroom?

Who is in our classroom today? *(Help students name all the people they see in the classroom. Have each student say the names of at least two people.)*

Individual Practice

(Provide individual practice.)

Part B: Read

It is my turn to read the story from this book. Remember, sit tall and listen big.
(While holding the book for students to see, read aloud pages 2–5. You may choose to replace pictures and names in the book with pictures of your students and their names, or you may wish to create your own selection.)

Now I will read the story again. This time, answer the questions with me. *(Reread aloud pages 2–5. Encourage students to answer the questions with you.)*

Part C: After Reading

We are going to practice saying the name of everyone in the story. *(Turn to the page 5.)*

My turn to say the names. *(Point to each picture.)* **Sally, Daniel, Brianna.**

Now let's say the names together. *(Call on students, pointing to each picture as each student says the name.)*
(Teacher and student:) **Sally, Daniel, Brianna**

Individual Practice

(Provide individual practice, pointing to each picture as each student says the name.)

We have finished all the parts of our lesson. Do you know what that means? It means I can put a sticker on your lesson Mastery Sheet! *(Put a sticker on the lesson Mastery Sheet, provide praise, and put away materials.)*

MATERIALS

1. Picture Magnets 1–4
2. Magnetic Marker Board
3. Letter-Sound Card 1 (Tt)
4. *Activity Book,* page 1

OBJECTIVES

Activity 1 *Rules*
- Establish rules

Activity 2 *Vocabulary*
- Preview how to take turns
- Say the names of objects represented by pictures

Activity 3 *Phonemic Awareness*
- Preview the first sound of a spoken word
- Say the first sound of a spoken word

Activity 4 *Letter Names*
- Learn the name of the letter *T*
- Associate names with letters

Activity 5 *Letter Names*
- Preview dots and how to trace
- Identify and write letters

Activity 1
Rules

(Review the following rules.)

Sit tall.
Listen big.

(Have students demonstrate each rule. You might need to prompt them by saying something like "Show me sitting tall.")

Remember, when you work hard and follow these rules, you will become better readers. I expect you to follow these rules every day. If you follow the rules, we will finish our lessons, and you will become good readers.

You have finished this activity, so I will make a check mark on the Mastery Sheet. Good job remembering the rules!

Activity 2
Picture Naming

Language and Literacy Support

Today I want to teach you a new word. The word is *turn*. When I ask a question, and each of you answers one at a time, this is called taking a turn.

When I want us to practice something we are learning, I will ask everyone to take a turn. What am I going to say if I want us to practice something we are learning? *(Accept reasonable responses.)*

That is right. If we are going to practice what we are learning, we will each take a turn practicing one at a time.

Good job!

We are going to look at some pictures of animals, and then we're going to name the animals.

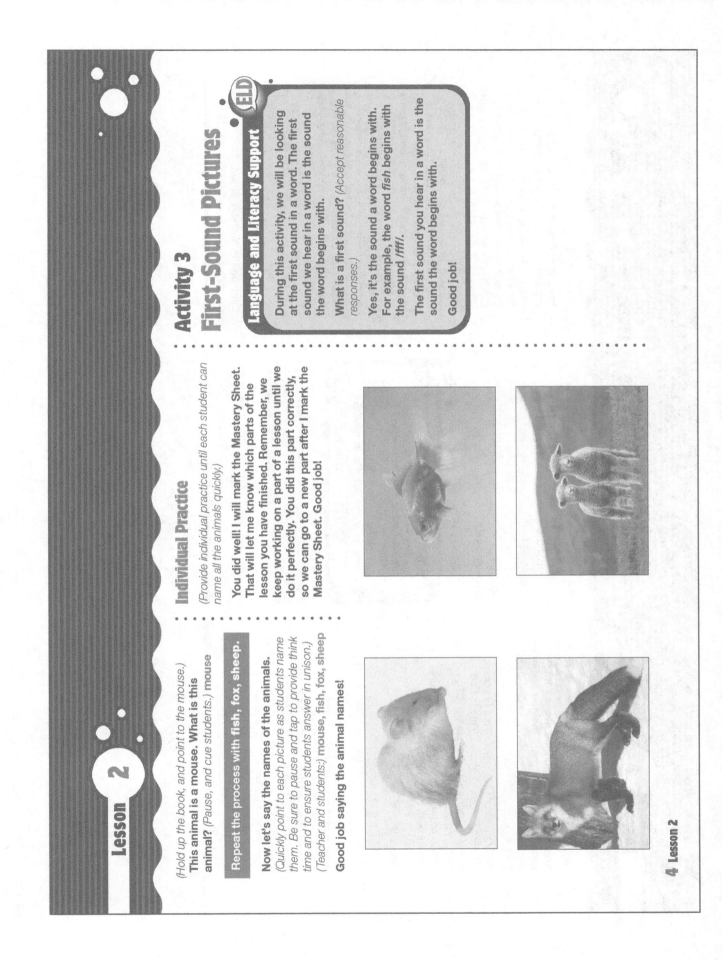

Lesson 2

(Hold up the book, and point to the mouse.)
This animal is a mouse. What is this animal? (Pause, and cue students.) mouse

Repeat the process with fish, fox, sheep.

Now let's say the names of the animals.
(Quickly point to each picture as students name them. Be sure to pause and tap to provide think time and to ensure students answer in unison.)
(Teacher and students:) mouse, fish, fox, sheep

Good job saying the animal names!

Individual Practice

(Provide individual practice until each student can name all the animals quickly.)

You did well! I will mark the Mastery Sheet. That will let me know which parts of the lesson you have finished. Remember, we keep working on a part of a lesson until we do it perfectly. You did this part correctly, so we can go to a new part after I mark the Mastery Sheet. Good job!

Activity 3
First-Sound Pictures

Language and Literacy Support

During this activity, we will be looking at the first sound in a word. The first sound we hear in a word is the sound the word begins with.

What is a first sound? (Accept reasonable responses.)

Yes, it's the sound a word begins with. For example, the word *fish* begins with the sound /fff/.

The first sound you hear in a word is the sound the word begins with.

Good job!

4 Lesson 2

Lesson 2

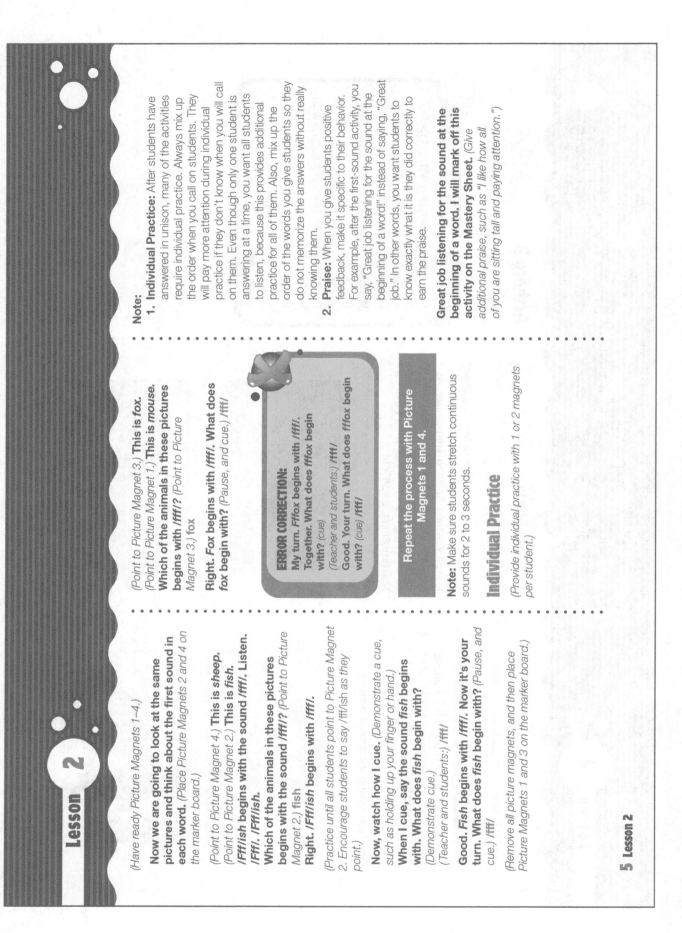

(Have ready Picture Magnets 1–4.)

Now we are going to look at the same pictures and think about the first sound in each word. (Place Picture Magnets 2 and 4 on the marker board.)

(Point to Picture Magnet 4.) **This is sheep.** (Point to Picture Magnet 2.) **This is fish. /Fff/ish begins with the sound /fff/. Listen. /fff/. /Fff/ish. Which of the animals in these pictures begins with the sound /fff/?** (Point to Picture Magnet 2.) fish **Right. /Fff/ish begins with /fff/.**

(Practice until all students point to Picture Magnet 2. Encourage students to say /fff/ish as they point.)

Now, watch how I cue. (Demonstrate a cue, such as holding up your finger or hand.) **When I cue, say the sound fish begins with. What does fish begin with?** (Demonstrate cue.) (Teacher and students:) /fff/

Good. Fish begins with /fff/. Now it's your turn. What does fish begin with? (Pause, and cue.) /fff/

(Remove all picture magnets, and then place Picture Magnets 1 and 3 on the marker board.)

(Point to Picture Magnet 3.) **This is fox.** (Point to Picture Magnet 1.) **This is mouse. Which of the animals in these pictures begins with /fff/?** (Point to Picture Magnet 3.) fox

Right. Fox begins with /fff/. What does fox begin with? (Pause, and cue.) /fff/

ERROR CORRECTION:

My turn. Fffox begins with /fff/.
Together. What does fffox begin with? (cue)
(Teacher and students:) /fff/
Good. Your turn. What does fffox begin with? (cue) /fff/

Repeat the process with Picture Magnets 1 and 4.

Note: Make sure students stretch continuous sounds for 2 to 3 seconds.

Individual Practice

(Provide individual practice with 1 or 2 magnets per student.)

Note:

1. **Individual Practice:** After students have answered in unison, many of the activities require individual practice. Always mix up the order when you call on students. They will pay more attention during individual practice if they don't know when you will call on them. Even though only one student is answering at a time, you want all students to listen, because this provides additional practice for all of them. Also, mix up the order of the words you give students so they do not memorize the answers without really knowing them.

2. **Praise:** When you give students positive feedback, make it specific to their behavior. For example, after the first-sound activity, you say, "Great job listening for the sound at the beginning of a word!" instead of saying, "Great job." In other words, you want students to know exactly what it is they did correctly to earn the praise.

Great job listening for the sound at the beginning of a word. I will mark off this activity on the Mastery Sheet. (Give additional praise, such as "I like how all of you are sitting tall and paying attention.")

5 Lesson 2

Lesson 2

Activity 4
Letter Introduction

(Hold up the **Tt** letter-sound card. Cover the lowercase t at the top of the card with a sticky note.)

(Point to the timer.) **Here is a picture of a timer. The word** *timer* **begins with** *T.* (Point to T.) **This letter is** *T.* **Say it with me when I touch it.** (Call on students. Pause, and cue.)
(Teacher and students:) T
Again. Say it with me.
(Teacher and students:) T

Individual Practice

(Provide individual practice.)

(Hold up the book. Point to Tom Tuttle.) **This says** *Tom Tuttle.* (Point to the T in Tom.) **There's a** *T* **at the beginning of** *Tom.* (Tap.) *T.*

When I point to the *T,* **say** *T.* (Call on students. Tap.) T
T **is also at the beginning of** *Tuttle.* **When I point to the** *T,* **say** *T.* (Call on students. Tap.) T

Tom Tuttle

6 Lesson 2

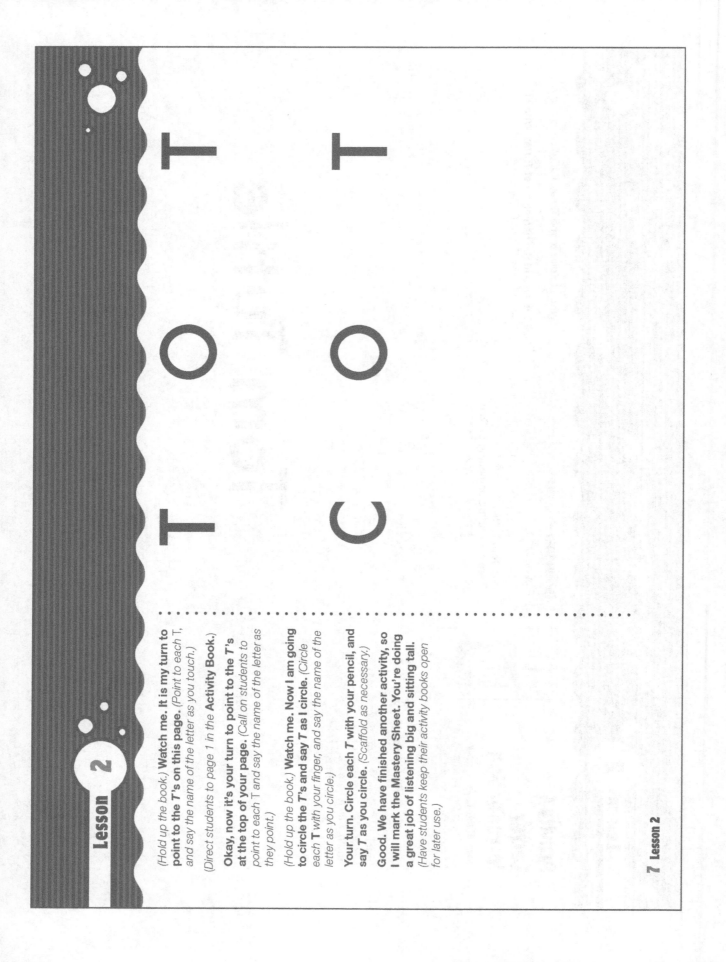

T   O   T

C   O   T

(Hold up the book.) Watch me. It is my turn to point to the T's on this page. *(Point to each T, and say the name of the letter as you touch.)*

(Direct students to page 1 in the **Activity Book.)**

Okay, now it's your turn to point to the T's at the top of your page. *(Call on students to point to each T and say the name of the letter as they point.)*

(Hold up the book.) Watch me. Now I am going to circle the T's and say T as I circle. *(Circle each T with your finger, and say the name of the letter as you circle.)*

Your turn. Circle each T with your pencil, and say T as you circle. *(Scaffold as necessary.)*

Good. We have finished another activity, so I will mark the Mastery Sheet. You're doing a great job of listening big and sitting tall. *(Have students keep their activity books open for later use.)*

Activity 5
Writing the Letter

Language and Literacy Support (ELD)

During this activity, we will be writing, and I want to make sure you understand everything I am talking about.

Who knows what a dot is? *(You may need to prompt further by saying:)* If I were to put a spot on your hand with this marker, what would that spot be? *(Accept reasonable responses.)*

That is right. A dot is a small spot or point, like this. *(Demonstrate drawing a dot on the marker board.)*

Good. Here's another question. What does it mean if I tell you to trace something? *(You may need to prompt further by saying:)* What if I tell you to trace the lines? *(Accept reasonable responses.)*

Yes. To trace means "to copy by connecting the dots," like this. *(Demonstrate tracing by drawing a dashed letter O on the marker board and then tracing the dashes.)*

Wonderful job!

(Hold up the Tt letter-sound card. Do not remove the sticky note from the lowercase t.)

Now we are going to learn how to write the letter T.

To write the letter T, we must write one line down *(trace in the air)* **and one line across** *(trace in the air).*

Now we are going to practice making a T in the air with our hands.

Watch me. My turn. Down *(trace in the air),* **across** *(trace in the air).* **T.**

Trace and say it with me.
(Teacher and students:) **down** *(trace in the air),* **across** *(trace in the air),* **T**

(Direct students to page 1 in the Activity Book.)

Now we are going to learn how to write the letter T. Watch how I write it. Say, "Down, across, T" with me as I write. *(Use your own activity sheet or the marker board, and refer to the letter formation guide in the back of the book.)*

(Teacher and students:) **down, across, T**

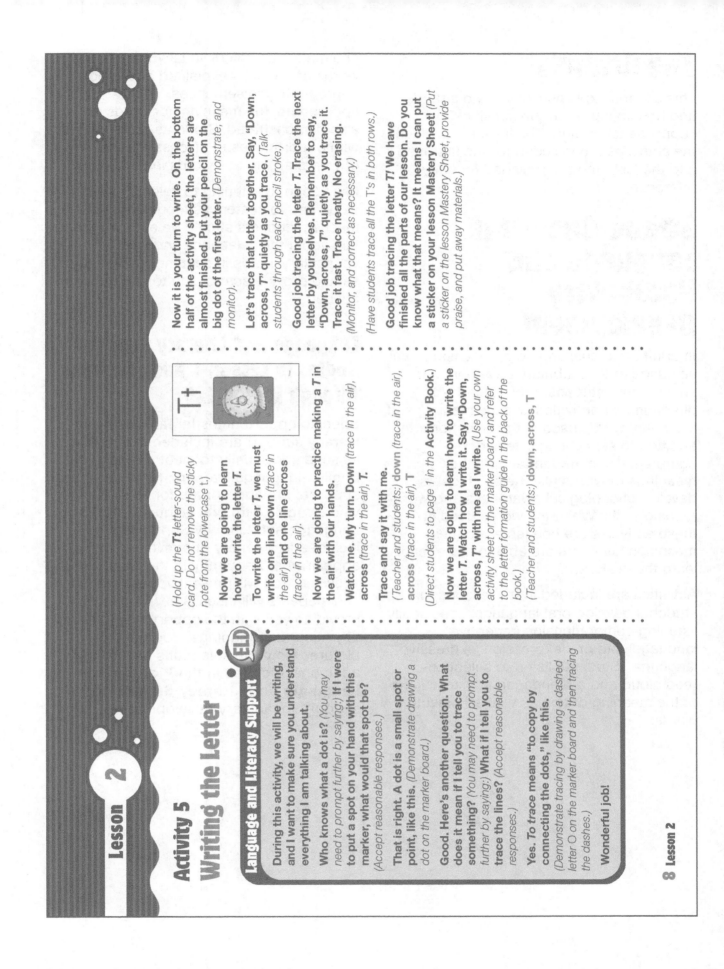

Now it is your turn to write. On the bottom half of the activity sheet, the letters are almost finished. Put your pencil on the big dot of the first letter. *(Demonstrate, and monitor).*

Let's trace that letter together. Say, "Down, across, T" quietly as you trace. *(Talk students through each pencil stroke.)*

Good job tracing the letter T. Trace the next letter by yourselves. Remember to say, "Down, across, T" quietly as you trace it. Trace it fast. Trace neatly. No erasing. *(Monitor, and correct as necessary.)*

(Have students trace all the T's in both rows.)

Good job tracing the letter T! We have finished all the parts of our lesson. Do you know what that means? It means I can put a sticker on your lesson Mastery Sheet! *(Put a sticker on the lesson Mastery Sheet, provide praise, and put away materials.)*

The Strands

This section explains each of the strands and how to carry out the activities that support each strand. The lessons in which the activities are included for the first time and the last time are provided for easy reference.

Strand One: Oral Language and Vocabulary Development

In addition to enabling comprehension, oral language and vocabulary development ensures that students understand directions for activities and the meanings of individual words used in the selections. In addition to supporting listening comprehension, understanding the meanings of words also helps students develop phonological awareness and word-reading skills. When the words used in these activities are connected to their meanings, students are able to more readily learn these skills.

Activities are included in the lessons to help students develop oral language, specifically listening comprehension (receptive language) and oral expression (expressive language). Students listen to selections read aloud and are engaged in discussions of the meaning of text as well as individual words.

The meanings of individual vocabulary words are directly explained and used appropriately in sentences. When appropriate, the meanings of words are also demonstrated. Students are provided with opportunities to discuss the meanings of words and to use words in sentences.

In addition to listening to selections read aloud and to sentences modeled by the teacher, students should be encouraged to talk about the selections and use vocabulary words in sentences. Teachers should provide scaffolding to students as needed.

Language and Literacy Support: Begins in Lesson 1 and continues through Lesson 120

Specific opportunities for language and literacy support are included in all of the lessons specifically to meet the needs of English-language learners; however, these supports are appropriate for all students who struggle with oral language. These Language and Literacy Supports are included in a variety of activities but appear most frequently in the Read-Aloud activities. You will present vocabulary words and students will discuss new vocabulary, providing you with the opportunity to clarify any misunderstandings. You will use pictures from the selections as well as additional pictures in the **Pictures for Language and Literacy Support** to support vocabulary development.

ACTIVITY AT A GLANCE

- Explain the meanings of vocabulary words, demonstrating when appropriate.
- Encourage students to discuss targeted vocabulary words, using the words in sentences and describing their meanings.
- Provide picture scaffolds to help students remember word meanings.

IN THE REAL WORLD

Although this section is designed for English-language learners, other students may also benefit from the additional vocabulary instruction and review, particularly students with intellectual disabilities, who typically experience language delays. Include vocabulary instruction for all students who need it, making sure that all students understand key vocabulary for the selection being read. When students understand the vocabulary, they can better understand the meaning of the selection. Most **Read-Aloud Book** selections are repeated across three different lessons, and vocabulary words are reviewed in each of these lessons. If your students are already familiar with the words highlighted, then you may prefer not to review them in subsequent lessons or you may simply review them very quickly.

Questions and Answers

Activity 1
Read-Aloud
Part A: Preview

ELD

Language and Literacy Support

During this activity, we will be reading a new story. I want to make sure you understand the story, so we are going to review some words.

The first word is *roam*. **Who knows what it means to roam?** *(If students give another meaning for the word that is also correct, acknowledge it, but focus on the contextual meaning used in the selection.)*

(You may need to prompt further by saying:) **What do I mean if I say *The dogs roam the park?*** *(Accept reasonable responses.)*

That's right! *To roam means "to walk around."* *(Demonstrate roaming around the classroom.)*

The next word is *perch.* **Does anyone know what a perch is?** *(If students give another meaning, acknowledge it, but focus on the meaning used in the selection.)*

(You may need to prompt further by saying:) **What do I mean if I say *A bird was looking down from his perch in the tree?*** *(Accept reasonable responses.)*

That's right! A perch is a branch or a stick where an animal sits. A perch is a high place where you can sit and watch something.

The next word is *lounge.* **Who knows what it means to lounge?** *(If students give another meaning, acknowledge it, but focus on the meaning used in the selection.)*

(You may need to prompt further by saying:) **What do I mean if I say *The cat likes to lounge on the couch doing nothing?*** *(Accept reasonable responses.)*

Yes! If I lounge somewhere, that means I spend time relaxing and sitting or lying down. *(Demonstrate lounging in your chair.)*

The last word is *stroll.* **Does anyone know what it means to stroll?** *(If students give another meaning, acknowledge it, but focus on the meaning used in the selection.)*

(You may need to prompt further by saying:) **What do I mean if I say *The family likes to stroll around the neighborhood?*** *(Accept reasonable responses.)*

That's right! If I stroll, that means I walk slowly. *(Demonstrate strolling around the classroom.)*

Excellent!

143 Lesson 33

Picture Naming: Begins in Lesson 2 and ends in Lesson 74

Students look at pictures and name them. Initially, students identify the pictures in unison as a group. Then, students are given opportunities to identify the pictures individually to ensure all students can name the pictures. The goal is for students to name the pictures quickly. Also, these same words will be used during phonological and phonemic awareness activities. Picture naming ensures that all students are familiar with these words prior to the phonological activities.

ACTIVITY AT A GLANCE

- Have students respond in unison to identify the pictures.

- Provide opportunities for individual students to identify the pictures.

IN THE REAL WORLD

Discuss the pictures and what they are as much as needed. Review meanings by quickly providing students with a sentence using that word. For students who already demonstrate mastery of Picture Naming, go through this activity very quickly, reducing or eliminating individual turns, and be sure to give the students appropriate praise.

Questions and Answers

Activity 2
Picture Naming

We are going to look at some pictures, and then we're going to name them.

(Hold up the book, and point to the pictures.)

The names of the pictures are *ship, nut, sun, lamp.*

Now say all the names of the pictures as I point to them.

(Quickly point to each picture, and have students name them. Be sure to pause and tap to provide think time and to ensure students answer in unison.)

(Teacher and students:) ship, nut, sun, lamp

Individual Practice

(Provide individual practice.)

You did well! That is another mark on the Mastery Sheet!

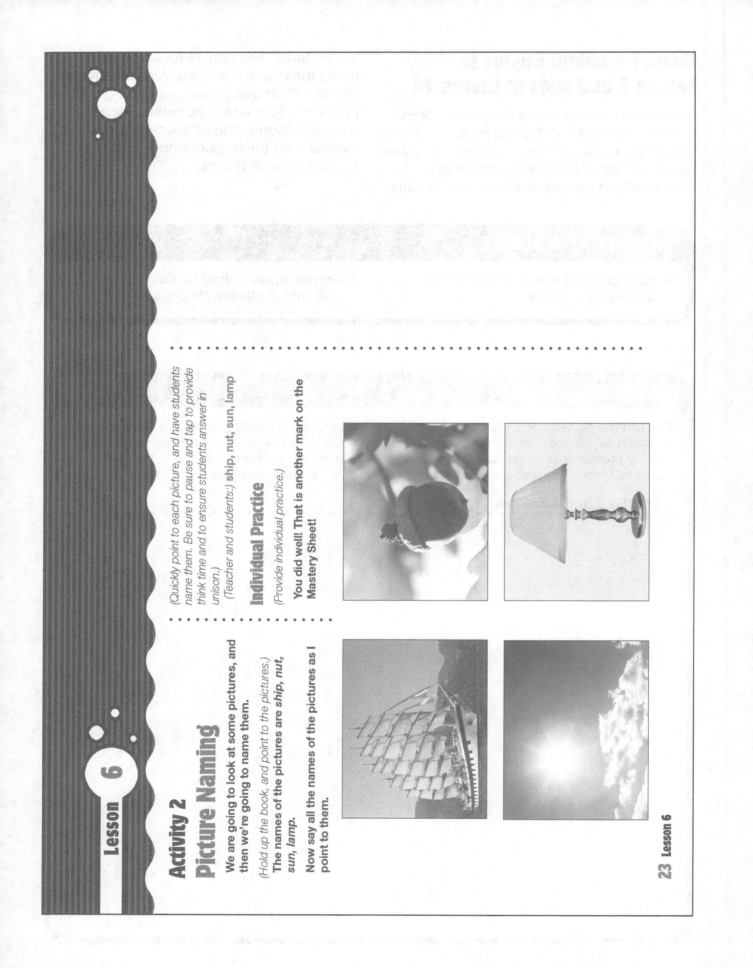

23 Lesson 6

Read-Aloud: Begins in Lesson 1 and ends in Lesson 119 (All Odd-Numbered Lessons)

The Read-Aloud activities are a critical component of the lessons, as they provide students with opportunities to use oral language to discuss texts, respond to questions, and use new vocabulary. How the Read-Aloud activities specifically address comprehension strategies is described in further detail in the following section describing Strand Two Comprehension Strategies.

Most **Read-Aloud** selections are read three times (in three different lessons). During the first lesson, previewing the text is emphasized. In the next Read-Aloud lesson, you stop periodically during the reading to discuss the meaning of the selection. The last time a selection is read, the selection is discussed after it is read in its entirety, allowing the students to enjoy the entire selection without interruptions and then demonstrate their understanding. Although dialogue is provided in the **Teacher's Editions** for how to teach Read-Aloud, use the dialogue as a flexible guide to help you address all the necessary skills and not as

a rigid script that must be followed verbatim. A primary purpose of this activity is to build oral language, both receptive (listening comprehension) and expressive language; therefore, it is critical that students are provided with opportunities to engage in discussion. Teachers should feel free to allow the discussion to develop naturally, using the script as a guide to support the conversation rather than as a set of questions that must be asked.

To use Read-Aloud activities to foster vocabulary development, focus on the highlighted vocabulary from the selections. Draw students' attention to the words before, during, and after reading. Provide opportunities before reading the text for students to define vocabulary and use the words in sentences. You will likely need to model appropriate sentences. Students may repeat your sentence or make up their own sentence, depending on their abilities. During reading, point out vocabulary in context and discuss meanings when necessary to improve comprehension. After reading, point out vocabulary again, and guide students to discuss how it was used in the selection.

ACTIVITY AT A GLANCE

- Before reading: Preview and define new vocabulary. Encourage discussion.
- During reading: Point out vocabulary in context. Review meanings when necessary. Encourage discussion.
- After reading: Discuss how new vocabulary was used in the selection.

IN THE REAL WORLD

Remember that the dialogue in the lessons is there as a guide and not as a strict verbatim script. The goal is to engage students in discussion about words and texts. If your students want to share connections they made with vocabulary or discuss other relevant ideas that are not explicitly mentioned in the lesson dialogue, follow their interests and deviate from the lesson dialogue.

For students who struggle with oral language, extend their responses and model appropriate speech each time they respond. For example, if a student defines a term with two words, praise the response and then rephrase it for the student, defining the term in a complete sentence to model appropriate oral language.

Questions and Answers

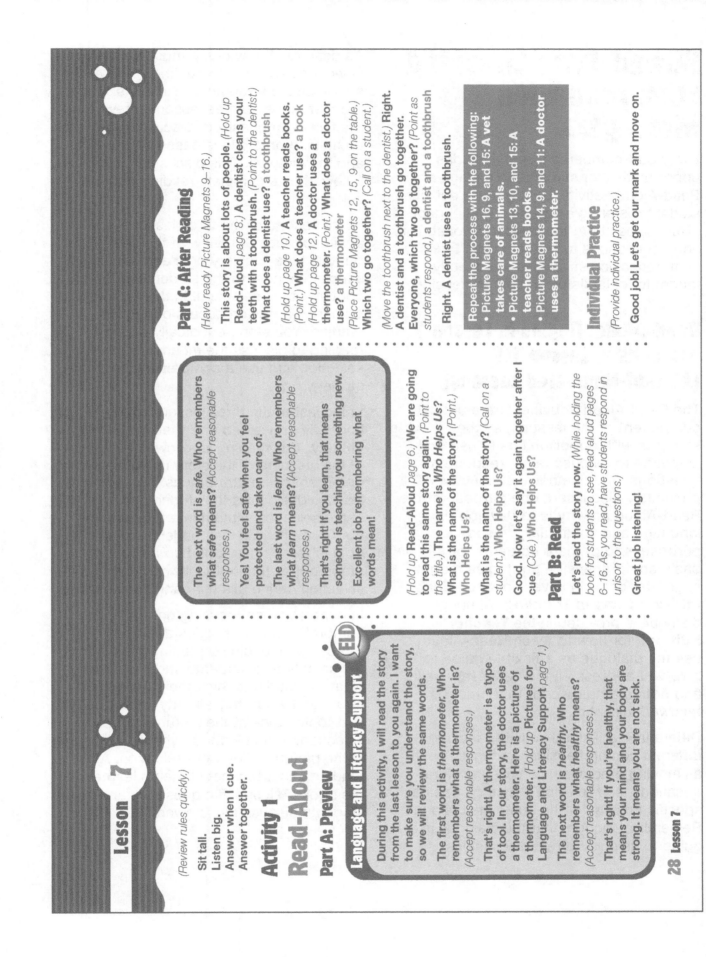

Lesson 7

(Review rules quickly.)

Sit tall.
Listen big.
Answer when I cue.
Answer together.

Activity 1
Read-Aloud

Part A: Preview

Language and Literacy Support (ELD)

During this activity, I will read the story from the last lesson to you again. I want to make sure you understand the story, so we will review the same words.

The first word is *thermometer.* Who remembers what a thermometer is? *(Accept reasonable responses.)*

That's right! A thermometer is a type of tool. In our story, the doctor uses a thermometer. Here is a picture of a thermometer. *(Hold up Pictures for Language and Literacy Support page 1.)*

The next word is *healthy.* Who remembers what *healthy* means? *(Accept reasonable responses.)*

That's right! If you're healthy, that means your mind and your body are strong. It means you are not sick.

The next word is *safe.* Who remembers what *safe* means? *(Accept reasonable responses.)*

Yes! You feel safe when you feel protected and taken care of.

The last word is *learn.* Who remembers what *learn* means? *(Accept reasonable responses.)*

That's right! If you learn, that means someone is teaching you something new.

Excellent job remembering what words mean!

(Hold up Read-Aloud page 6.) We are going to read this same story again. *(Point to the title.)* The name is *Who Helps Us?* What is the name of the story? *(Point.)* Who Helps Us?

What is the name of the story? *(Call on a student.)* Who Helps Us?

Good. Now let's say it again together after I cue. *(Cue.)* Who Helps Us?

Part B: Read

Let's read the story now. *(While holding the book for students to see, read aloud pages 6–16. As you read, have students respond in unison to the questions.)*

Great job listening!

Part C: After Reading

(Have ready Picture Magnets 9–16.)

This story is about lots of people. *(Hold up Read-Aloud page 8.)* A dentist cleans your teeth with a toothbrush. *(Point to the dentist.)* What does a dentist use? a toothbrush

(Hold up page 10.) A teacher reads books. *(Point.)* What does a teacher use? a book *(Hold up page 12.)* A doctor uses a thermometer. *(Point.)* What does a doctor use? a thermometer

(Place Picture Magnets 12, 15, 9 on the table.) Which two go together? *(Call on a student.)*

(Move the toothbrush next to the dentist.) Right. A dentist and a toothbrush go together. Everyone, which two go together? *(Point as students respond.)* a dentist and a toothbrush

Right. A dentist uses a toothbrush.

Repeat the process with the following:
- Picture Magnets 16, 9, and 15: **A vet takes care of animals.**
- Picture Magnets 13, 10, and 15: **A teacher reads books.**
- Picture Magnets 14, 9, and 11: **A doctor uses a thermometer.**

Individual Practice

(Provide individual practice.)

Good job! Let's get our mark and move on.

28 Lesson 7

Strand Two: Listening Comprehension Strategies

Every odd-numbered lesson includes opportunities for students to engage in a Read-Aloud activity. During these activities students listen to a selection and engage in discussions about the selection, vocabulary, and connections to the selection. Basic comprehension strategies are directly taught to foster listening comprehension.

Read-Aloud: Begins in Lesson 1 and ends in Lesson 119 (All Odd-Numbered Lessons)

The Read-Aloud activities are a critical component of the lessons, as they provide students with opportunities to use oral language to discuss texts, respond to questions, and use new vocabulary. As previously discussed, one purpose of the Read-Aloud activity is to develop oral language and vocabulary. A second purpose is to prepare students for the basic comprehension strategies taught in greater detail in Level 1 of *SRA Early Interventions in Reading.* Although dialogue is provided in the **Teacher's Editions** for how to teach Read-Aloud, use the dialogue as a flexible guide to help you address all the necessary skills and not as a rigid script that must be followed verbatim.

Different Read-Aloud activities include different comprehension strategies, such as making predictions, answering literal questions, and retelling the story. See each specific activity for the complete dialogue. Remember, though, that the dialogue is a guide to help you direct discussions.

As described previously, most **Read-Aloud** selections are read three times in three successive odd-numbered lessons. During the first of these three lessons, previewing the text is emphasized. Discussion focuses on making predictions based on the title and the pictures. This discussion is typically followed by a complete reading of the selection.

In the second of the three lessons, you again conduct a preview of the selection, but this time it is very brief and serves as a simple reminder to the students of the basic content of the selection. In this lesson, the primary discussion occurs during the reading. You stop periodically during the reading to discuss the meaning of the selection and use a comprehension strategy.

In the last of the three lessons, the selection is briefly previewed and then read in its entirety. This reading is followed by a review of the meaning of the story using the same comprehension strategy as the second lesson. This allows the students to enjoy the entire selection without interruptions and then demonstrate their understanding. The goal is for the previous two lessons to prepare the student to fully comprehend the selection during this third and final reading.

In general, when focusing on comprehension strategies during Read-Aloud, begin by reading the title of the selection to students and discussing what the students think the story will be about and what they already know about that topic. Look at the pictures in the selection, and talk about what is happening in the pictures. Read the selection. After reading, discuss what students learned in the book. Ask specific questions and have students discuss the answers.

ACTIVITY AT A GLANCE

- Before reading: Make predictions based on the story title. Do a picture walk: look at the pictures and discuss what is happening. (This discussion is emphasized the first time a selection is read. See Lesson 89.)

- During reading: Point out vocabulary in context. Review meanings when necessary. Discuss the meaning of the selection using the targeted comprehension strategy. Students will likely require support for comprehension. (This discussion is emphasized the second time a selection is read. See Lesson 91.)

- After reading: Discuss the meaning of the story using the targeted comprehension strategy. The goal is for students to answer questions more independently (i.e., with less scaffolding and support). (This discussion is emphasized the third and final time the selection is read. See Lesson 93.)

IN THE REAL WORLD

Remember that the dialogue in the lessons is there as a guide and not as a strict verbatim script. The goal is to engage students in talks about the selection. If your students want to share connections they made with vocabulary or discuss other relevant ideas that are not explicitly mentioned in the lesson dialogue, follow their interests and divert from the lesson dialogue.

For students who struggle with oral language, extend their responses and model appropriate speech each time they respond. For example, if a student answers a question with two words, praise the response, and rephrase it for the student, answering the question in a complete sentence to model appropriate oral language.

Questions and Answers

MATERIALS

1. *Read-Aloud*, pages 256–289

OBJECTIVES

Activity 1 *Comprehension Strategies*
(ELD) Recognize the meanings of words
- Browse a selection to make a prediction
- Comprehend text read orally
- Answer literal questions about the text
- Retell a selection in order of events

Activity 2 *Concepts of Print*
- Recognize word placement in sentences

Activity 1
Read-Aloud

Language and Literacy Support (ELD)

During this activity, we will be reading a new story. I want to make sure you understand the story, so we are going to review some words.

The first word is *delicious.* Does anyone know what *delicious* means? *(If students give another meaning for the word that is also correct, acknowledge it, but focus on the contextual meaning used in the selection.)*

(You may need to prompt further by saying:) **What do I mean if I say *My grandmother makes the most delicious chocolate cake?* (Accept reasonable responses.)**

That's right! *Delicious* means "tastes very, very good."

The next word is *follow.* Does anyone know what *follow* means? *(If students give another meaning, acknowledge it, but focus on the meaning used in the selection.)*

(You may need to prompt further by saying:) **What do I mean if I say *My dogs follow me around the house?* (Accept reasonable responses.)**

That's right! If you follow someone, that means you walk right behind them.

The next word is *leap.* Who knows what *leap* means? *(If students give another meaning, acknowledge it, but focus on the meaning used in the selection.)*

(You may need to prompt further by saying:) **What do I mean if I say *The frogs leap from one lily pad to another?* (Accept reasonable responses.)**

Yes! *To leap* means "to jump." *(Demonstrate leaping.)*

The last word is *naughty.* Who knows what *naughty* means? *(If students give another meaning, acknowledge it, but focus on the meaning used in the selection.)*

(You may need to prompt further by saying:) **What do I mean if I say *The naughty child would not listen to her parents?* (Accept reasonable responses.)**

Yes! If you are naughty, that means you are doing something you are not supposed to do.

Nice work on these words!

Lesson 89

(Hold up **Read-Aloud** pages 256 and 257.) **We are going to read a new story.** (Point to the title.) **The title is Ginger.**

What is the title of the story? (Point.) Ginger

Note: Use this format for the **Read-Aloud** selection. The goals are for students to increase sentence length and use a wider vocabulary.

Preview

1. **Predict:** Flip through the selection with students, asking them to comment on what is happening in the pictures.

2. **Discuss:** Ask guiding questions, such as **What do you think Ginger is? Do you think Ginger is a boy cat or a girl cat?** (Do not reveal the cat's gender until the story is read.) **Whom do you see? What are they doing? How do they feel?**

3. **Vocabulary:** Preteach the terms *curl up, fast asleep,* and *spring.*

Read

1. While holding the book for students to see, read aloud pages 256–289.

After Reading

2. **Discuss:** Ask the following questions: **Were our guesses about the story correct? Is Ginger a boy cat or a girl cat? How does Ginger feel when the girl brings home the kitten? How does Ginger feel at the end of the story? What did you like about the story?**

3. **Oral Story Retell:** Guide students in retelling the selection in order. Scaffold by asking guiding questions as needed. The focus should be on selection discussion rather than on sequencing the selection correctly.

   • Extend language by modeling the use of sequencing words, such as *first, next, beginning,* and *end.*

ERROR CORRECTION:
If students speak in short sentences or do not speak in complete sentences, expand on their language by telling them a sentence that uses as many of their words as possible. Then have the student repeat the sentence. If students are highly engaged, spend a few minutes modeling longer sentences and having students repeat the sentences.

Great job listening to the story about Ginger the cat! I'll give you a check mark.

Lesson 91

MATERIALS

1. *Read-Aloud*, pages 256–289

OBJECTIVES

Activity 1 *Comprehension Strategies*
- Recognize the meanings of words
- Comprehend text read orally
- Answer literal questions about the text
- Retell a selection in order of events

Activity 2 *Concepts of Print*
- Recognize word placement in sentences

Activity 1
Read-Aloud

Language and Literacy Support

ELD

In this lesson, I will read the story from the last lesson to you again. I want to make sure you understand the story, so we are going to review the same words.

The first word is *delicious*. Does anyone remember what *delicious* means? *(Accept reasonable responses.)*

That's right! *Delicious* means "tastes very, very good."

The next word is *follow*. Does anyone remember what *follow* means? *(Accept reasonable responses.)*

That's right! If you follow someone, that means you walk right behind them.

The next word is *leap*. Who remembers what *leap* means? *(Accept reasonable responses.)*

Yes! *To leap* means "to jump." *(Demonstrate leaping.)*

The last word is *naughty*. Who remembers what *naughty* means? *(Accept reasonable responses.)*

Yes! If you are naughty, that means you are doing something you are not supposed to do.

Nice work remembering the meanings of these words!

(Hold up **Read-Aloud** *page 256.)* **We are going to read about Ginger the cat again.** *(Point to the title.)* **The title is** *Ginger.*

What is the title of the story? *(Point.)* Ginger

Lesson 91

Note: Use this format for the *Read-Aloud* selection. The goals are for students to increase sentence length and use a wider vocabulary.

Preview

1. **Discuss:** Say **What do you remember about the story?** Scaffold as needed, flipping through the selection with students, showing the pictures.
   - Ask guiding questions, such as **How does Ginger feel at the beginning of the story? How does Ginger feel when the girl brings home the kitten? How does Ginger feel at the end of the story?**

2. **Vocabulary:** Reteach the terms *curl up, fast asleep,* and *spring.*

Read

1. **Oral Story Retell:** While holding the book for students to see, begin to read aloud pages 256–289.
   - Stop reading as needed to sequence events. Ask **What happened first/next/last?** as you read each part of the story. Scaffold by asking guiding questions as needed. The focus should be on selection discussion rather than on sequencing the selection correctly.
   - Extend language by modeling the use of sequencing words, such as *first, next, beginning,* and *end.*

Great job listening to the story about Ginger the cat! I'll give you a check mark.

63 Lesson 91

Lesson 93

MATERIALS

1. *Read-Aloud*, pages 256–289

OBJECTIVES

Activity 1 *Comprehension Strategies*
(ELD) Recognize the meanings of words
- Comprehend text read orally
- Answer literal questions about the text
- Retell a selection in order of events

Activity 2 *Concepts of Print*
- Recognize word placement in sentences

Activity 1
Read-Aloud

Language and Literacy Support (ELD)

In this lesson, I will read the story from the last lesson to you again. I want to make sure you understand the story, so we are going to review the same words.

The first word is *delicious*. Does anyone remember what *delicious* means? *(Accept reasonable responses.)*

That's right! *Delicious* means "tastes very, very good."

The next word is *follow*. Does anyone remember what *follow* means? *(Accept reasonable responses.)*

That's right! If you follow someone, that means you walk right behind them.

The next word is *leap*. Who remembers what *leap* means? *(Accept reasonable responses.)*

Yes! To *leap* means "to jump." *(Demonstrate leaping.)*

The last word is *naughty*. Who remembers what *naughty* means? *(Accept reasonable responses.)*

Yes! If you are naughty, that means you are doing something you are not supposed to do.

Nice work remembering the meanings of these words!

(Hold up **Read-Aloud** *page 256.)* **We are going to read about Ginger the cat again.** *(Point to the title.)* **The title is** *Ginger.*

What is the title of the story? *(Point.)* Ginger

Note: Use this format for the *Read-Aloud* selection. The goal is for students to increase sentence length and use a wider vocabulary.

Preview

1. **Discuss:** Say **What do you remember about the story?** Scaffold as needed, flipping through the selection with students, showing the pictures and asking guiding questions.

2. **Vocabulary:** Reteach the terms *curl up, fast asleep,* and *spring.*

Read

1. While holding the book for students to see, read aloud pages 256–289.

Lesson 93

After Reading

1. Oral Story Retell: Guide students in retelling the selection in order. Scaffold by asking guiding questions as needed. The focus should be on selection discussion rather than on sequencing the selection correctly.

• Extend language by modeling the use of sequencing words, such as *first, next, beginning,* and *end.*

ERROR CORRECTION:
If students speak in short sentences or do not speak in complete sentences, expand on their language by telling them a sentence that uses as many of their words as possible. Then have the student repeat the sentence. If students are highly engaged, spend a few minutes modeling longer sentences and having students repeat the sentences.

You've earned a check mark for doing so well with our story.

76 Lesson 93

Strand Three: Phonological Awareness

Phonological awareness is the awareness that oral language consists of words and that words consist of sounds. Phonemic awareness, the awareness of the phonemes that make up spoken words, is a component of phonological awareness. However, Strand Three focuses on the larger units of phonological awareness (words and syllables), and a separate strand, Strand Four, focuses specifically on phonemic awareness. Phonological awareness activities included in the lessons that help students recognize words and syllables are Say and Move, Syllable Clapping, and Rhyme Time.

Say and Move: Begins in Lesson 3 and ends in Lesson 13

Through Say and Move, students learn that sentences have words and that reading is done from left to right. To do Say and Move, read a sentence from the **Read-Aloud Book** to the students. Then have students say the sentence with you. Next, set out blank magnets, one for each word that is in the sentence. Say the sentence again, but this time, push a magnet up as you say each word in the sentence. Pass out blank magnets or squares to the students. Together, push the squares up while saying each word in the sentence. Next, provide individual practice by having each student say at least one sentence, moving a square or magnet for each word of the sentence. Remember, the purpose is for students to understand that a spoken sentence has multiple words in it.

ACTIVITY AT A GLANCE

- Step 1: Read a sentence from the **Read-Aloud Book.**
- Step 2: Have students say the sentence with you.
- Step 3: Set out blank squares or magnets, one per word in the sentence.
- Step 4: Say the sentence, this time pushing up one square for each word as you say the word.
- Step 5: Pass out blank squares or magnets to the students.
- Step 6: Have students say each word in the sentence with you while pushing up one square for each word.
- Step 7: Provide individual practice with each student for at least one sentence.

IN THE REAL WORLD

Remember to use blank squares, not cards with words on them. The goal of this activity is for students to learn that sentences are made up of words. They do not have to be able to read the words from the sentence, so use blank squares as manipulatives.

You can use your magnetic marker board for this activity, or just put the magnets or squares on the table. If you have small magnetic boards for each student, you can use those as well. Be sure to keep your supplies close to you so you can reach them without interrupting the pace of your lesson or losing the students' attention.

Questions and Answers . . . .

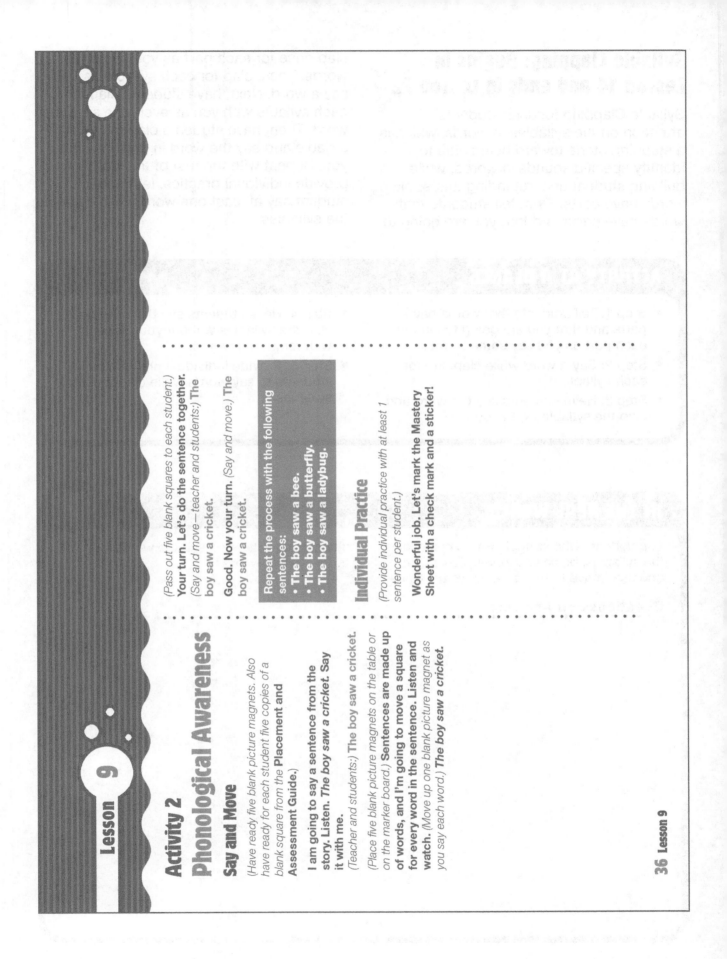

Lesson 9

Activity 2
Phonological Awareness

Say and Move

(Have ready five blank picture magnets. Also have ready for each student five copies of a blank square from the Placement and Assessment Guide.)

I am going to say a sentence from the story. Listen. *The boy saw a cricket.* **Say it with me.**

(Teacher and students:) **The boy saw a cricket.**

(Place five blank picture magnets on the table or on the marker board.) **Sentences are made up of words, and I'm going to move to a square for every word in the sentence. Listen and watch.** *(Move up one blank picture magnet as you say each word.)* **The boy saw a cricket.**

(Pass out five blank squares to each student.) **Your turn. Let's do the sentence together.** *(Say and move—teacher and students:)* **The boy saw a cricket.**

Good. Now your turn. *(Say and move.)* **The boy saw a cricket.**

> Repeat the process with the following sentences:
> • **The boy saw a bee.**
> • **The boy saw a butterfly.**
> • **The boy saw a ladybug.**

Individual Practice

(Provide individual practice with at least 1 sentence per student.)

Wonderful job. Let's mark the Mastery Sheet with a check mark and a sticker!

36 Lesson 9

Syllable Clapping: Begins in Lesson 14 and ends in Lesson 22

Syllable Clapping focuses students' attention on the syllables in words, which is a stepping stone toward being able to identify specific sounds in words, while building student understanding that spoken words have parts. First, tell students that words have parts and that you are going to clap once for each part as you say some words. Then, clap for each syllable as you say a word. Next, have students clap for each syllable with you as everyone says the word. Then, have students clap for each syllable and say the word in unison without you. Repeat with the rest of the words. Last, provide individual practice, letting each student say at least one word while clapping the syllables.

ACTIVITY AT A GLANCE

- Step 1: Tell students that words have parts and that you are going to clap for each part as you say some words.
- Step 2: Say a word while clapping for each syllable.
- Step 3: Have students say the word and clap the syllables with you.

- Step 4: Have students say the word and clap the syllables without you. Repeat with remaining words.
- Step 5: Provide individual practice for students to say words while clapping the syllables.

IN THE REAL WORLD

For students who struggle with differentiating the syllables, begin with one-syllable words, and then move to two-syllable words. Once students can clap two-syllable words, add three-syllable words.

Questions and Answers

Lesson 16

Activity 5
Phonological Awareness

Syllable Clapping

Note: For this activity, if students appear unsure of the word meanings, show them Picture Magnets 26–29, 32, and 33.

Words are made up of parts. I am going to say some words. I will clap once for each word part. My turn. Listen. (Clap once for each word part.) **But/ter/fly. Listen again.** (Clap once for each word part.) **But/ter/fly.**

Let's try it together.
(Say and clap—teacher and students:) but/ter/fly

By yourselves. (Say and clap.) but/ter/fly

Very good! Let's move on to the next word.

ERROR CORRECTION:
If students make an error, use the model-lead-test strategy.

Repeat the process with the following words: **ze/bras, crick/et, la/dy/bug, bee, mouse.**

Individual Practice
(Provide individual practice with 1 or 2 words per student.)

Very well done. Time to put a check mark on the Mastery Sheet.

64 Lesson 16

Rhyme Time: Begins in Lesson 24 and ends in Lesson 34

Rhyme Time helps students listen for ending sounds in words. Use picture magnets to help students understand the vocabulary used in the activity. You say a word and point to a picture magnet of that word. Put two picture magnets below the first magnet, one that rhymes and one that does not. Tell the students the two words as you point to each magnet. Ask students which one rhymes with the first word. Tell students which word rhymes and what the ending sound is. Practice saying the rhyming words together. Remove the two bottom magnets, and do the same activity again with the first magnet and the same words. Once students have successfully responded with those words, continue the activity with three new magnets and new words, then again with more new words. Provide individual practice with at least one set of the words used in that day's activity.

ACTIVITY AT A GLANCE

- Step 1: Tell students they will learn how words rhyme, and define *rhyme.*
- Step 2: Show one picture magnet and say the corresponding word.
- Step 3: Place two magnets below the first magnet and say the corresponding words.
- Step 4: Ask students which one of the two words rhymes with the first word.
- Step 5: Tell students which one of the words rhymes and what the ending sound is.
- Step 6: Repeat steps 2 through 4 with the same magnets and the same words.
- Step 7: Once students can correctly respond, repeat steps 2 through 4 with new pictures and words.
- Step 8: Repeat steps 2 through 4 again with more new pictures and words.
- Step 9: Provide individual practice with at least one set of words.

IN THE REAL WORLD

For students who struggle to hear the ending sounds, provide additional modeling, emphasizing the ending sound when you say the words.

Questions and Answers

Lesson 30

Activity 4
Phonological Awareness

Rhyme Time

(Have ready Picture Magnets 1, 20, 37, 39, 40, 43, 50, 54, and 61.)

Now it's Rhyme Time. Remember, when words rhyme, the end of each word sounds the same. Listen carefully.

Your turn. *(Place Picture Magnet 61 near the top of the board. Point.)* **This is jar.** *(Place Picture Magnets 37 and 39 on the board below Picture Magnet 61. Point.)* **This is cat.** *(Point.)* **This is car.**

Which word rhymes with jar? car Right. Car rhymes with jar because they both end with /arr/.

Good job. Let's practice some more.

Repeat the process with the following:
- **Picture Magnets 54 (bell), 40 (light), 20 (shell)**
- **Picture Magnets 50 (fan), 1 (mouse), 43 (man).**

> **ERROR CORRECTION:**
> If students make an error, use the model-lead-test strategy.

Individual Practice

(Provide individual practice with at least 1 set of picture magnets per student until each student correctly chooses the 2 words in the set that rhyme.)

Good job. I'll mark the Mastery Sheet.

131 Lesson 30

Strand Four: Phonemic Awareness

Phonemic awareness is the awareness of the phonemes that make up spoken words. It is the aspect of phonological awareness that focuses on the smallest meaningful unit of sound, the phoneme. Two critical phonemic awareness skills are blending and segmenting. Blending is combining sounds in order to make a whole word. Segmenting is separating a word into its individual sounds. Blending phonemes lays the foundation for being able to sound out new words. Segmenting phonemes lays the foundation for being able to spell new words. Several blending and segmenting activities are included in the lessons.

Segmenting

First-Sound Pictures: Begins in Lesson 2 and ends in Lesson 16

Distinguishing the beginning sound of a word is the easiest of the phoneme segmentation skills, so it is the first phonemic awareness activity in the lessons.

As an additional scaffold, students look at pictures of the words being said to give them a visual of the word being manipulated in the activity.

To do First-Sound Pictures, tell your students they will be listening for the first sound in each word. Two pictures at a time, show pictures, and tell students the names of the pictures, emphasizing the first sound. Emphasize the sound by stretching it. All of the words in the First-Sound Pictures activity begin with continuous sounds and can be stretched. This helps the students hear the sound clearly. Then, tell students the beginning sound of one of the pictures, and ask students which picture begins with that sound. Continue the activity with additional sets of two pictures. Provide individual practice.

ACTIVITY AT A GLANCE

- Step 1: Show two pictures, and tell students to listen for the beginning sounds of the words you say.
- Step 2: Say the words, emphasizing the beginning sound of each word.
- Step 3: Tell students the beginning sound of one picture, and ask students which picture begins with that sound. Students respond in unison with your cue.
- Step 4: Repeat the activity with two different pictures until all pairs of pictures have been used.
- Step 5: Provide individual practice.

IN THE REAL WORLD

If students struggle with articulation, have them point to the correct picture as they say the word.

Questions and Answers

Activity 2
First-Sound Pictures

Stretching

(Have ready Picture Magnets 2, 17, 18, 20, and 21.)

Now we are going to think about the first sound in each word. *(Place Picture Magnets 20 and 21 on the marker board.)*

(Point to Picture Magnet 20.) **This is *shell*.**
(Point to Picture Magnet 21.) **This is *moon*.**
Listen. */mmm/*. Which of the things in these pictures begins with */mmm/?* moon
Right. *Moon* begins with */mmm/*.

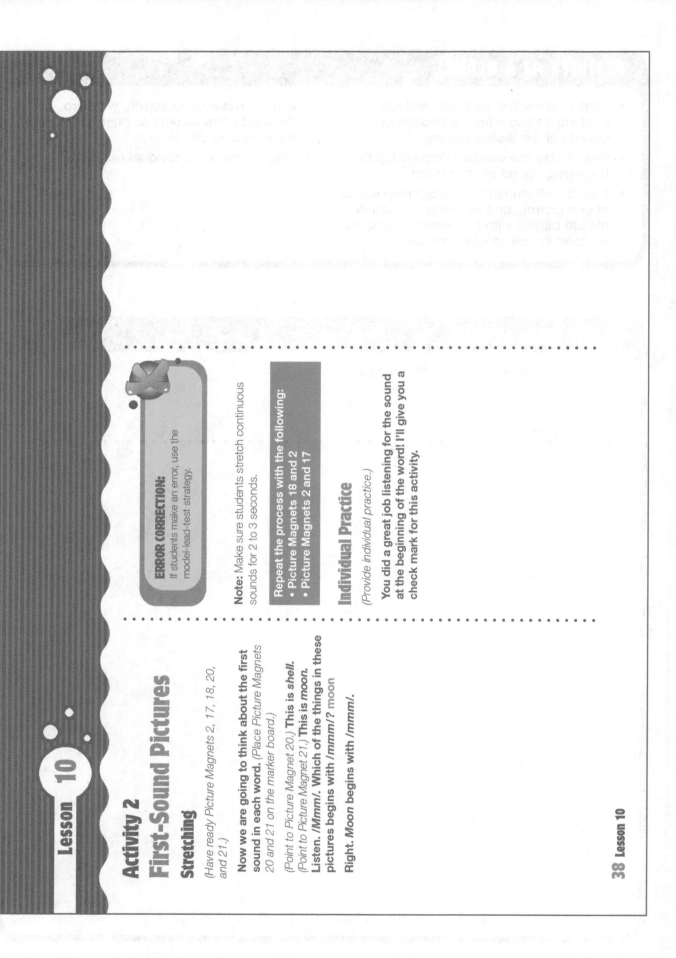

ERROR CORRECTION:
If students make an error, use the model-lead-test strategy.

Note: Make sure students stretch continuous sounds for 2 to 3 seconds.

Repeat the process with the following:
• **Picture Magnets 18 and 2**
• **Picture Magnets 2 and 17**

Individual Practice

(Provide individual practice.)

You did a great job listening for the sound at the beginning of the word! I'll give you a check mark for this activity.

First-Sound Game: Begins in Lesson 10 and ends in Lesson 40

First-Sound Game focuses on identifying the first phoneme in a spoken word. To play First-Sound Game, say a word. When the first sound is a continuous sound, hold the sound for two or three seconds. Then, cue with your finger to signal for students to respond by saying the first sound in the word. Model the first word for them, and then do the first word again all together. Next, say a new word, and have students respond in unison. Continue the activity with the rest of the words. Then provide opportunities for individual practice.

ACTIVITY AT A GLANCE

- Step 1: Say a word, holding the first sound for two or three seconds when it is a continuous sound.
- Step 2: Tell students what the first sound is.
- Step 3: Say the word again. This time have the students respond with you.
- Step 4: Say a new word. Have students respond in unison by saying the first sound.
- Step 5: Repeat step 4 with the rest of the words.
- Step 6: Provide individual practice.

IN THE REAL WORLD

Emphasize the beginning sound and hold it out longer for students who struggle to hear the beginning sound. Earlier lessons include only words that begin with continuous sounds. As lessons progress, words beginning with stop sounds are also included. Remember that this activity is reviewed again in the next few lessons. You can continue to the next lesson as long as students are making progress with the activity, even if they do not master it fully in one lesson.

Questions and Answers

Activity 3

First-Sound Game

Now we are going to play the First-Sound Game. We are going to listen for the first sound we hear in a word. I'll say a word. When I cue, you tell me the first sound you hear in the word. I'll do one first.

(Hold the first sound 2–3 seconds.) **My turn. Fish. What's the first sound in fish?** *(Hold up one finger.)* **/Fff/.**

Now it's your turn. I'll say a word. When I cue, tell me the first sound you hear. First word. Mail. What's the first sound in mail? *(Cue.)* **/mmm/**
Yes, good listening. Next word.

Note: Make sure students stretch continuous sounds for 2 to 3 seconds.

Repeat the process with the following words: /sh/ell, /rrr/ain, /mmm/oon.

Individual Practice

(Provide individual practice.)

I'll mark the Mastery Sheet!

47 **Lesson 12**

Stretch-the-Word Game: Begins in Lesson 54 and continues through Lesson 120

Stretch-the-Word Game extends First-Sound Game and requires students to identify all the sounds in the word instead of just the first sound. This skill is continued in Level 1. To play Stretch-the-Word Game, say a word. First, model for the students how to stretch a word by saying the word slowly, stretching continuous sounds. Continuous sounds should be held for two or three seconds. Each time you say a sound, hold up one finger to represent the new sound. Next, have students stretch the same word with you to practice the activity. Then have students stretch new words without you. Once all the words have been stretched in unison, provide opportunities for independent practice.

ACTIVITY AT A GLANCE

- Step 1: Say a word.
- Step 2: Model for students how to stretch the word. Hold continuous sounds for two or three seconds. Each time you say a new sound, hold up one finger to represent the new sound.
- Step 3: Say the word again. This time have the students stretch the word with you.
- Step 4: Say the word again. This time have the students stretch the word without you.
- Step 5: Say a new word. Have students respond in unison by stretching the word and representing the phonemes with their fingers.
- Step 6: Repeat step 5 with the rest of the words.
- Step 7: Provide individual practice.

IN THE REAL WORLD

Be careful to hold up a finger when you say a new sound. Holding up your finger too early or too late can be confusing for the students. Holding continuous sounds for even longer than three seconds can be helpful for students who struggle to hear the different phonemes. It also helps students who struggle to model connecting sounds. In other words, say each sound and keep saying that sound until you start saying the next sound. Do not stop between sounds.

Questions and Answers

Activity 3

Stretch-the-Word Game

Now you are going to stretch words the way Maxwell does. We played this game once before. It's called Stretch the Word. Remember, I will say a word, and you will tell me the sounds you hear in the word.

Watch how I do it. First, I hold up my fist. *(Demonstrate.)* Next, I slowly say each sound I hear in a word, and I hold up one finger as I say each sound.

My turn to do the first word. **Sew.** I'll stretch *sew. (Hold up one finger for each sound.)* **/Sss/ /ōōō/.**

Now you stretch the word *(pause) sew (pause)* with me. Fists up. **Sew.** *(Pause.)* **Stretch sew.** *(Teacher and students:)* **/sss/ /ōōō/**

Excellent! Now stretch by yourselves. **Sew.** *(Pause.)* **Stretch sew. /sss/ /ōōō/**

Individual Practice

(Provide individual practice.)

Here is a word to stretch. We'll do this one together. *(Pause.)* **Shoe.** *(Pause.)* **Stretch shoe.**
(Teacher and students:) **/sh/ /ōō/**

Now by yourselves. Shoe. *(Pause.)* **Stretch shoe. /sh/ /ōō/**

(Practice until all students can stretch shoe, following your finger cue as a group.)

Individual Practice

(Provide individual practice.)

Here's another word to stretch. We will do this one together. Knee. *(Pause.)* **Stretch knee.**
(Teacher and students:) **/nnn/ /ēēē/**

Now by yourselves. Stretch knee. /nnn/ /ēēē/

Here's one more word to stretch. Let's see if you can do this one by yourselves the first time. Fists up. Moo. *(Pause.)* **Stretch moo. /mmm/ /ōō/**

Individual Practice

(Provide individual practice with 1 or 2 words per student.)

You have done another great job on this part of the lesson. I'll check off this section on the Mastery Sheet.

Stop-and-Go Game: Segmenting: Begins in Lesson 70 and ends in Lesson 120

Stop-and-Go is a game designed to allow students to practice blending and segmenting phonemes. The game does include letters, allowing students to practice applying blending and segmenting to printed words. Although students practice letter-sound correspondences, sounding out words, and spelling words, the primary purpose of the game is to learn to blend and segment spoken words quickly and easily. That way, as students learn new letter-sounds later, they will be able to blend the sounds and sound out words made up of the new letter-sounds. There are three levels of difficulty: Red, Yellow, and Green. Each level is played in the same way but with different letter cards and therefore with different words to build.

To play Stop-and-Go: Segmenting, divide the students into two teams. Teams take turns responding and moving around the board until one team reaches the stoplight. Teams take turns responding, but you should encourage all students to think of the correct response every time.

The segmenting version of the game has two main steps.

Step 1: Hold up a letter card and have the team identify the letter-sound. The team moves two spaces for a go sound and one space for a stop sound. Then it is the other team's turn. Teams continue taking turns and identifying letter-sounds until you have letters that build a word. When you can build a word, continue to Step 2.

Step 2: Tell students the word, and have the students stretch the word, cueing students by holding up one finger for each sound in the word. Ask all students to be thinking of the spelling. Ask the same student who identified the last sound to build the word by moving the letters to spell the word on the Build-a-Word Mat.

Each time you complete Step 2, repeat Step 1 until a new word can be built. The game stops when one team reaches the stoplight.

ACTIVITY AT A GLANCE

- Step 1: Divide students into two teams that take turns responding, but encourage all students to think of the correct responses every time.

- Step 2: Turn over a letter card. One team identifies the letter-sound. The team moves 2 spaces if it is a go sound and 1 space if it is a stop sound.

- Step 3: When enough letter cards have been turned over to build a word, have everyone stretch the word, holding out go sounds and saying stop sounds quickly. Have the last student to turn over a letter build the word by moving letters to the Build-a-Word Mat.

- Step 4: Everyone stretches the word with you, holding up one finger each time a new sound is spoken.

- Step 5: Everyone says the word fast.

- Step 6: Repeat Steps 2 through 5 until one team reaches the stoplight at the end of the board.

IN THE REAL WORLD

If students struggle, simply model the correct response and have students repeat the correct response. Students always move around the board even if you have to model a correct answer for them.

Questions and Answers

Lesson 70

Activity 8
Stop-and-Go Game

Red Level: Segmenting

Note: In Lesson 70, the game switches in Step 2 from blending to segmenting.

(Have ready the Stop-and-Go Game Board, Stop-and-Go Mat, Build-a-Word Mat, Red Level letter cards, and game tokens.)

(Shuffle the Red Level letter cards and place them in a pile facedown near the game board. Divide the class into two teams.)

Step 1: Sound Pronunciation

It's time to play the Stop-and-Go Game! *(Draw and hold up a Red Level letter card.)* **Everybody, think. What is this letter's sound?** *(Call on a student.)* **The sound is _____. Everybody, say it with me.** *(Scaffold as needed.)* **Good. The sound _____ is a [stop or go] sound.** *(Have the same student move 1 or 2 spaces, depending on whether the sound is continuous or stop.)*

Repeat Step 1, calling on students from both teams, until there are enough letters to build one of the following words: **am, Sam, at, fat, mat, sat.**

Step 2: Stretching the Word

(Once you have enough letters to build a word, ask for students' attention.)

Everybody, think. *(Call on the same student who identified the last letter-sound. Tell the student to build the word by moving those letters to build the word on the Build-a-Word Mat. Scaffold as needed by saying each sound. Scaffold further as needed by pointing to the letters.)*

Good! *(Call on the same student.)* **Stretch this word. Fist up.** *(Point to each letter. Scaffold as needed.)*

What word? *(Scaffold as needed.)*
Great work! My turn. Listen to me. *(Point to each letter. Stretch the word and then say it fast.)* **Everybody, stretch the word with me. Fists up.** *(Point to each letter. Scaffold as needed.)*

Everybody, what word? *(Say the word fast.)*
Yes! *(Have the same student move 2 spaces.)*

Great work, everybody. Now I will draw another card.

Each time you complete Step 2, repeat Step 1 until a new word can be built. Draw cards, build and stretch words, and move tokens until one team reaches the stoplight at the end of the game board.

(Congratulate the team who won the game by moving the team's token to the stoplight.)

Good job playing the Stop-and-Go Game! Time for both a check mark and a sticker!

Blending

Say-the-Word Game: Begins in Lesson 4 and ends in Lesson 120

A puppet named Maxwell is provided to use during Say the Word. Maxwell can say words only in a funny way; he says words slowly so every sound in the word can be heard. Maxwell is sure to hold continuous sounds for two or three seconds and to say stop sounds quickly without distorting the sound. Students listen to Maxwell and try to figure out the word he says.

ACTIVITY AT A GLANCE

- Step 1: If you have not already done so, introduce Maxwell to the students. Tell the students that Maxwell says words in a funny way. Ask your students to teach Maxwell to speak better by saying the words fast.
- Step 2: Move Maxwell's mouth and say a word slowly, holding continuous sounds for two or three seconds and saying stop sounds quickly without distorting the sound.
- Step 3: Ask your students what word Maxwell said.
- Step 4: Repeat the procedure with the remaining words.
- Step 5: Provide individual practice.

IN THE REAL WORLD

Sometimes students leave off a sound or invert sounds when they blend the sounds back into a word. Be sure to listen carefully to your students' responses and model correct blending when necessary.

Questions and Answers

Develop a personality for Maxwell as you use him. He can be a motivational tool for keeping students engaged in the lesson.

Activity 4
Oral Blending
Say-the-Word Game

(Use Maxwell the puppet to say words in stretched form.)

This is Maxwell. Remember him? He can say words only in a funny way. Whenever he says a word, he stretches it. You have to tell me what word he said.

(Whisper to Maxwell:) **Maxwell, what is the first word?**

(Speaking through Maxwell:) /Nnn/ut

What word did Maxwell say? nut

Yes, *nut.*

Repeat the process with the following words: /sh/ip, /lll/amp, /sss/un.

ERROR CORRECTION:
If students make an error, gradually shorten the length of the first sound.

Individual Practice

(Provide individual practice with 1 or 2 words per student.)

Great job listening to Maxwell! That's another check on the Mastery Sheet.

Stop-and-Go Game: Blending: Begins in Lesson 62 and ends in Lesson 118

Stop-and-Go is a game designed to allow students to practice blending and segmenting phonemes. The game does include letters, allowing students to practice applying blending and segmenting to printed words. Although students practice letter-sound correspondences, sounding out words, and spelling words, the primary purpose of the game is to learn to blend and segment spoken words quickly and easily. That way, as they learn new letter-sounds later, students will be able to blend the sounds and sound out words made up of the new letter-sounds. There are three levels of difficulty: Red, Yellow, and Green. Each level is played the same, but with different letter cards, and therefore with different words to build.

Stop-and-Go: Blending is played in the same manner as the segmenting version, except that when a word can be built, the teacher moves the letter cards to show the students the word and the students blend the letter-sounds to sound out the word.

To play Stop-and-Go: Blending, divide the students into two teams. Teams take turns responding and moving around the board until one team reaches the stoplight first. Teams take turns responding, but you should encourage all students to think of the correct response every time.

The blending version of the game has two main steps.

Step 1: Hold up a letter card and have the team identify the letter-sound. If it is a go sound, the team moves two spaces. If it is a stop sound, the team moves one space. Then it is the other team's turn. Continue taking turns and identifying letters until you have letters that build a word. When you can build a word, continue to Step 2.

Step 2: Put the word on the Build-a-Word Mat. Ask all students to be thinking of the word. Call on the student who drew the last letter to say the sounds in the word slowly, stretching go sounds and saying stop sounds quickly. Then have the students say the word fast. Next, have everyone stretch the word with you, holding up one finger each time a new sound is said. Last, have everyone say the word fast again.

Each time you complete Step 2, repeat Step 1 until a new word can be built. The game stops when one team reaches the stoplight at the end of the board.

ACTIVITY AT A GLANCE

- Step 1: Divide students into two teams that take turns responding, but encourage all students to think of the correct responses every time.
- Step 2: Turn over a letter card. Call on a student from one team to identify the letter-sound. The team moves 2 spaces for each go sound and 1 space for each stop sound.
- Step 3: When enough letter-sounds have been identified to build a word, move the word to the Build-a-Word Mat. Have the student who identified the last letter-sound say the sound of each letter in the word, holding out go sounds and saying stop sounds quickly.
- Step 4: Then have the student say the word fast.
- Step 5: Everyone stretches the word with you, holding up one finger each time a new sound is spoken.
- Step 6: Everyone says the word fast.
- Step 7: Repeat Steps 2 through 6 until one team reaches the stoplight.

IN THE REAL WORLD

Any time students struggle, simply model the correct response. If students struggle to blend the word, make sure they do not stop between sounds.

Questions and Answers

Activity 6

Stop-and-Go Game

Red Level: Blending

(Before this activity, read the Stop-and-Go Game Booklet. Familiarize yourself with the Red Level game rules, as well as the alternate game options, if desired.)

(Have ready the Stop-and-Go Game Board, Stop-and-Go Mat, Build-a-Word Mat, Red Level letter cards, and game tokens.)

(Shuffle the Red Level letter cards and place them in a pile facedown near the game board. Divide the class into two teams.)

We are going to play a reading game together. This game is called the Stop-and-Go Game. I've divided you into two teams. Each team is going to take turns moving around the board. We'll see which team gets to the stoplight first! I'll show you how to play as we go.

During the game, we are going to practice saying sounds and words. Anytime you do not know a sound or a word, I will tell you the sound or word, so listen carefully! Before we start, I want to make sure you understand what a stop sound is and what a go sound is.

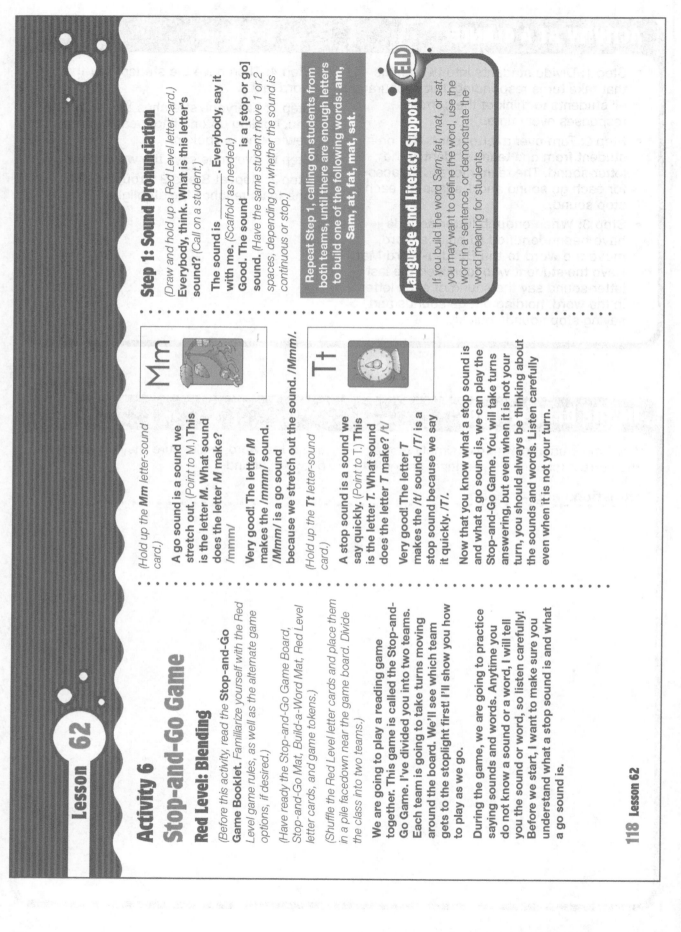

(Hold up the Mm letter-sound card.)

A go sound is a sound we stretch out. *(Point to M.)* This is the letter M. What sound does the letter M make? /mmm/

Very good! The letter M makes the /mmm/ sound. /Mmm/ is a go sound because we stretch out the sound. /Mmm/.

(Hold up the Tt letter-sound card.)

A stop sound is a sound we say quickly. *(Point to T.)* This is the letter T. What sound does the letter T make? /t/

Very good! The letter T makes the /t/ sound. /T/ is a stop sound because we say it quickly. /T/.

Now that you know what a stop sound is and what a go sound is, we can play the Stop-and-Go Game. You will take turns answering, but even when it is not your turn, you should always be thinking about the sounds and words. Listen carefully even when it is not your turn.

Step 1: Sound Pronunciation

(Draw and hold up a Red Level letter card.) Everybody, think. What is this letter's sound? *(Call on a student.)*

The sound is _____. Everybody, say it with me. *(Scaffold as needed.)* Good. The sound _____ is a [stop or go] sound. *(Have the same student move 1 or 2 spaces, depending on whether the sound is continuous or stop.)*

Repeat Step 1, calling on students from both teams, until there are enough letters to build one of the following words: **am, at, fat, mat, sat.**

Language and Literacy Support

If you build the word *Sam, fat, mat,* or *sat,* you may want to define the word, use the word in a sentence, or demonstrate the word meaning for students.

Lesson 62

Step 2: Sound Blending

(When you have enough letters to build a word, move those letters to spell the word on the Build-a-Word Mat.)

Everybody, think. *(Call on the same student who identified the last letter-sound.)* **Look at this word. Say the sounds in this word slowly. Make sure you stretch all the go sounds and say all the stop sounds quickly. Do not stop between sounds. Fist up.** *(Point to each letter. Scaffold as needed.)* **What word?** *(Scaffold as needed.)*

Great work! My turn. Listen to me. *(Point to each letter. Stretch the word and then say it fast.)* **Everybody, stretch the word with me. Fists up.** *(Point to each letter. Scaffold as needed.)* **Everybody, what word?** *(Say the word fast.)* **Yes!** *(Have the same student move 2 spaces.)* **Great work, everybody. Now I will draw another card.**

Each time you complete Step 2, repeat Step 1 until a new word can be built. Draw cards, build and stretch words, and move tokens until one team reaches the stoplight at the end of the game board.

(Congratulate the team who won the game by moving the team's token to the stoplight.)

Excellent job playing the Stop-and-Go Game! I will check off this activity on the Mastery Sheet and also give you a sticker for the lesson.

TEACHER'S GUIDE

RED LEVEL

Go Sounds	Stop Sounds
/aaa/	/t/
/fff/	
/mmm/	
/sss/	

Word List
am
Sam
at
fat
mat
sat

Strand Five: Letter Names

In order to talk about letters, letter-sounds, how to spell words, and how to read words, it is important for students to be able to identify the names of letters quickly and easily.

Letter Introduction: Begins in Lesson 2 and ends in Lesson 104

In Letter Introduction, students are taught new letter names with the aid of a letter-sound card that illustrates the letter. For example, *T* is introduced using a card with *Tt* on the top and a picture of Tom Tuttle's Timer beneath the letters.

To introduce a new letter name, show the letter-sound card to the students, and tell them what it is a picture of and what letter it begins with. Then tell them what the letter is. Have students say the letter with you multiple times as you tap the card to cue their unison response. Next, provide individual opportunities for students to point to the letter in the words and say the name of the letter.

ACTIVITY AT A GLANCE

- Step 1: Show the letter-sound card to the students. Tell them what it is a picture of and what letter they are learning.
- Step 2: Point to the letter on the top of the card, and tell students what the letter is.
- Step 3: Have students say the name of the letter in unison when you tap the card to cue their response.
- Step 4: Have students point to the letter in words and say its name.
- Step 5: Have students individually point to the letter and say its name. Give each student multiple turns.

IN THE REAL WORLD

For students who struggle with this activity, use magnetic letter manipulatives.

Questions and Answers

Activity 4
Letter Introduction

*(Hold up the **Oo** letter-sound card.)*

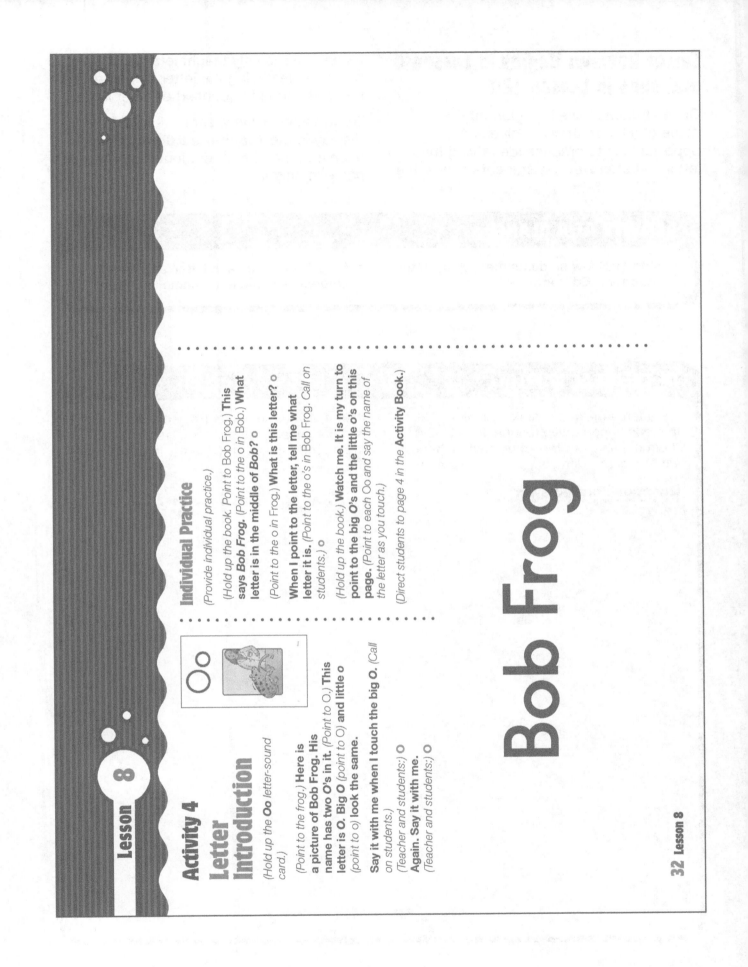

(Point to the frog.) **Here is a picture of Bob Frog. His name has two O's in it.** *(Point to O.)* **This letter is O. Big O** *(point to O)* **and little o** *(point to o)* **look the same.**

Say it with me when I touch the big O. *(Call on students.)*

(Teacher and students:) O
Again. Say it with me.
(Teacher and students:) O

Individual Practice

(Provide individual practice.)

(Hold up the book. Point to Bob Frog.) **This says Bob Frog.** *(Point to the o in Bob.)* **What letter is in the middle of Bob?** o

(Point to the o in Frog.) **What is this letter?** o

When I point to the letter, tell me what letter it is. *(Point to the o's in Bob Frog. Call on students.)* o

(Hold up the book.) **Watch me. It is my turn to point to the big O's and the little o's on this page.** *(Point to each Oo and say the name of the letter as you touch.)*

(Direct students to page 4 in the Activity Book.)

Bob Frog

Letter Review: Begins in Lesson 4 and ends in Lesson 120

Once students have been taught the name of a letter, they are given many opportunities to practice identifying the letter. In Letter Review, students review the name of a recently taught letter and practice identifying the letter by name, both by itself and in the context of other letters.

To do Letter Review, show students the display in the **Teacher's Edition.** Point to each letter, and have students say the letter name in unison.

ACTIVITY AT A GLANCE

- Step 1: Show students the display in the **Teacher's Edition.**

- Step 2: Point to each letter, and have students say the letter name in unison.

IN THE REAL WORLD

If students make a mistake, provide immediate corrective feedback by telling them the name of the letter, having them say the name with you, and then having them tell you the name. Back up two items and continue the activity to give students the opportunity to practice the missed item again.

Questions and Answers

Lesson 46

Activity 5
Letter Review

(Hold up the book.) **Let's practice letter names we have learned. Remember, when I point to a letter, say its name.**

(Point to n.) **n**

(Point to each letter, remembering to move from left to right across the page.)

ERROR CORRECTION:
If students make an error, use the model-lead-test strategy. If students say the sound of a letter, rather than its name, say **Yes, that is the sound that letter makes. But what is the name of that letter?**

Individual Practice
(Provide individual practice.)
You're doing a great job. I'll mark the Mastery Sheet.

33 Lesson 46

Writing the Letter: Begins in Lesson 2 and ends in Lesson 104

There are many benefits to knowing how to write letters. Not only is it important for being able to write in a way that others can read your message, but practice with writing letters also supports learning letter names when the letter name is spoken during writing. Later, as the sounds are taught, they can be reinforced in this manner as well. Each lesson that includes instruction or practice with letter names also includes opportunities for students to write the letter.

To introduce how to write a letter, first tell the students the name of the letter they will learn to write. Moving your finger in the air, model how to write the letter while describing orally what to do and saying the letter name. For example, while making a *t* in the air with your finger, say **down, across, t.** Then have students do it with you, while everyone says what to do and the name of the letter. Pass out the **Activity Books** and pencils. Model how to write the letter on paper or on the marker board, saying how to write the letter and the name of the letter. Have students trace and write the letter in their books as they softly say how to write and the name of the letter.

ACTIVITY AT A GLANCE

- Step 1: Tell students the name of the letter they will write.
- Step 2: Model how to write the letter in the air with your finger, while saying what to do to write the letter and the name of the letter.
- Step 3: Everyone writes the letter in the air with fingers, while saying what to do and the name of the letter.

- Step 4: Pass out **Activity Books** and pencils.
- Step 5: Model how to write the letter on paper while saying what to do to write the letter and the name of the letter.
- Step 6: Have students trace and write the letter in their **Activity Books** while softly saying what to do and the name of the letter.

IN THE REAL WORLD

For preschool students who struggle with the fine motor skills to write, reduce the number of times they have to write in the **Activity Book** in order to prevent frustration.

For students with disabilities that prevent them from being able to write, write for them as they dictate to you what to write. Students may also find the correct letters from a small set of magnetic letters that includes several target letters and several distracter letters. (For example, if the target letter is *t*, include several *t*'s and several other letters.)

Questions and Answers

Lesson 2

Activity 5
Writing the Letter

Language and Literacy Support 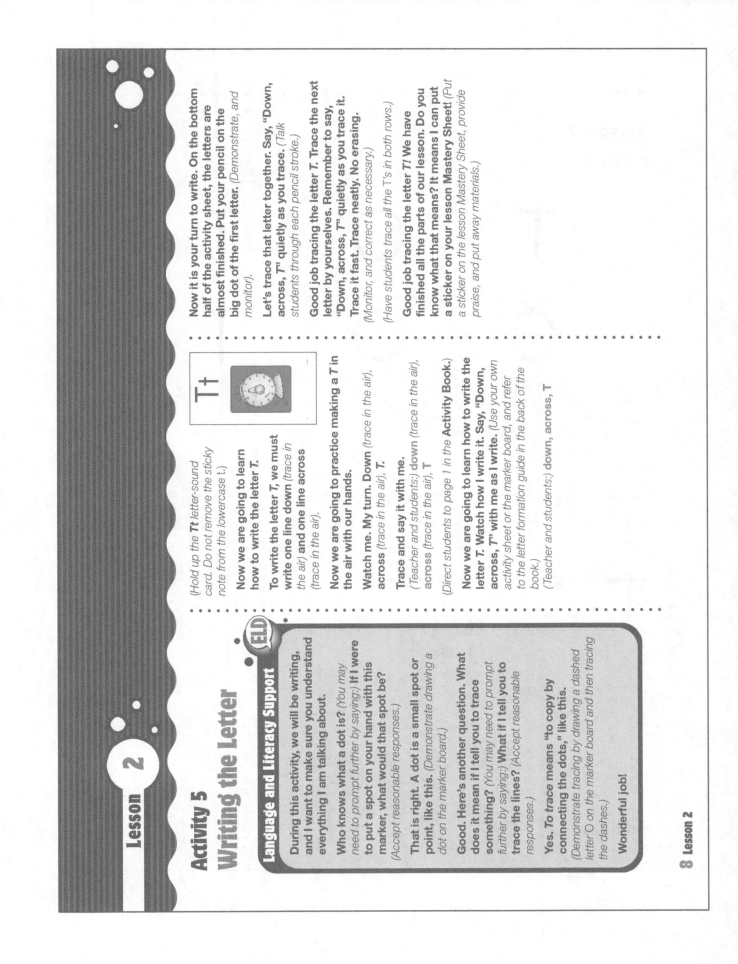 ELD

During this activity, we will be writing, and I want to make sure you understand everything I am talking about.

Who knows what a dot is? *(You may need to prompt further by saying:)* If I were to put a spot on your hand with this marker, what would that spot be? *(Accept reasonable responses.)*

That is right. A dot is a small spot or point, like this. *(Demonstrate drawing a dot on the marker board.)*

Good. Here's another question. What does it mean if I tell you to trace something? *(You may need to prompt further by saying:)* What if I tell you to trace the lines? *(Accept reasonable responses.)*

Yes. To trace means "to copy by connecting the dots," like this. *(Demonstrate tracing by drawing a dashed letter O on the marker board and then tracing the dashes.)*

Wonderful job!

(Hold up the Tt letter-sound card. Do not remove the sticky note from the lowercase t.)

Now we are going to learn how to write the letter T.

To write the letter T, we must write one line down *(trace in the air)* and one line across *(trace in the air).*

Now we are going to practice making a T in the air with our hands.

Watch me. My turn. Down *(trace in the air),* across *(trace in the air),* T.

Trace and say it with me.
(Teacher and students:) down *(trace in the air),* across *(trace in the air),* T

*(Direct students to page 1 in the **Activity Book**.)*

Now we are going to learn how to write the letter T. Watch how I write it. Say, "Down, across, T" with me as I write. *(Use your own activity sheet or the marker board, and refer to the letter formation guide in the back of the book.)*

(Teacher and students:) down, across, T

Now it is your turn to write. On the bottom half of the activity sheet, the letters are almost finished. Put your pencil on the big dot of the first letter. *(Demonstrate, and monitor).*

Let's trace that letter together. Say, "Down, across, T" quietly as you trace. *(Talk students through each pencil stroke.)*

Good job tracing the letter T. Trace the next letter by yourselves. Remember to say, "Down, across, T" quietly as you trace it. Trace it fast. Trace neatly. No erasing. *(Monitor, and correct as necessary.)*

(Have students trace all the T's in both rows.)

Good job tracing the letter T! We have finished all the parts of our lesson. Do you know what that means? It means I can put a sticker on your lesson Mastery Sheet! *(Put a sticker on the lesson Mastery Sheet, provide praise, and put away materials.)*

8 Lesson 2

Name_____

Lesson 2

Activity 4

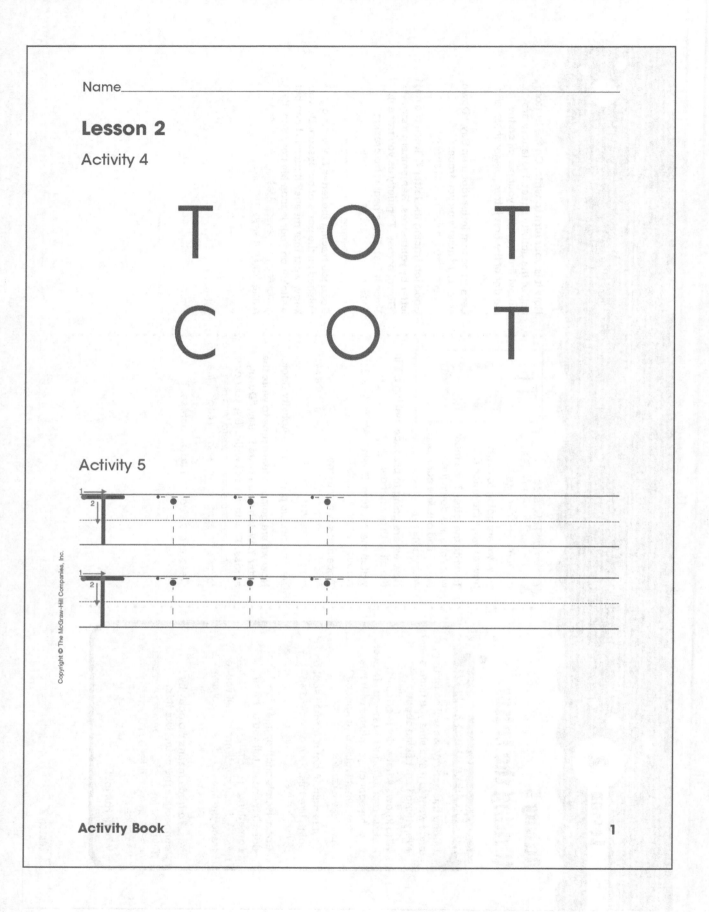

T O T

C O T

Activity 5

Activity Book

1

Writing the Letter Review: Begins in Lesson 4 and ends in Lesson 104

Once students have been taught how to write a new letter, they are given many opportunities to practice writing both the capital and the lowercase versions of the letter. First, review how to write the letter, and model writing the letter in the air with your finger. Next, pass out **Activity Books** and pencils. Have students trace and write the letter in the **Activity Books** while saying how to write the letter and the name of the letter.

ACTIVITY AT A GLANCE

- Step 1: Review how to write the letter.
- Step 2: Model how to write the letter in the air with your finger while saying what to do to write the letter and the name of the letter.

- Step 3: Pass out **Activity Books** and pencils.
- Step 4: Have students trace and write the letter in their **Activity Books** while softly saying what to do and the name of the letter.

IN THE REAL WORLD

In order to keep students motivated, offer them a variety of cute pencils or colored pencils when practicing writing.

Questions and Answers . . . .

Activity 7
Writing the Letter

Now we are going to practice writing S's. Remember, to write a big S and a little s, we put one hand in the air and move it around this way and around that way. *(Trace in the air.)* Around, around, S.

Trace and say it with me.
(Teacher and students:) around *(trace in the air)*, around *(trace in the air)*, S

(Direct students to page 8 in the Activity Book.)

Now we are going to write the big S and the little s. Watch how I write it. Say S with me as I write. *(Use your own activity sheet or the marker board.)*
(Teacher and students:) S

Now it is your turn to trace a big S on your activity sheet. Remember to say S quietly as you trace it. Trace fast. Trace neatly. No erasing. *(Monitor, and correct as necessary.)*

Great job tracing the big letter S. Now let's do the little s. Trace this letter by yourselves.

(Monitor, and correct as necessary.)

Great job. Now let's finish the page. As you trace, say the name of the letter quietly.

(Have students trace the remainder of the page. Monitor, and correct as necessary.)

You have done an excellent job on this activity. I'll mark the Mastery Sheet, and I'll also put a sticker on the Mastery Sheet because we're done with the lesson!

Name _____

Lesson 16

Activity 7

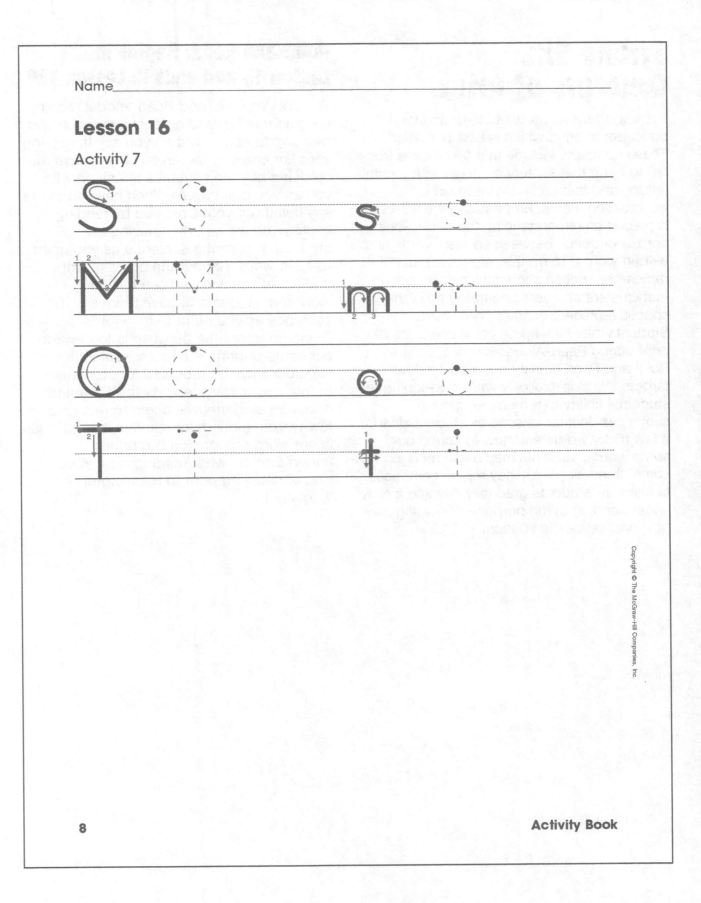

8

Activity Book

Strand Six: Concepts of Print

It is important for students to understand concepts of print, which is how print works. These concepts include that text moves from left to right, that sentences begin with capital letters, and that sentences end with punctuation marks. Emphasis in the lessons is placed on understanding the one-to-one correspondence between spoken words and written words. To do this, students must remember spoken sentences and recognize that clusters of letters separated by blank spaces represent each spoken word. Students may pick up on other concepts of print during Read-Aloud activities, but the Point and Read activity described below targets this skill explicitly while developing the students' ability to remember spoken sentences. In later lessons as students learn a few tricky words and how to sound out some words, students may begin recognizing some of the words as they repeat sentences. In this way, students gradually develop a clear understanding of the purpose of reading and how print relates to speech.

Point and Read: Begins in Lesson 15 and ends in Lesson 120

To conduct Point and Read, model reading for students by reading each sentence and pointing to each word as you say it, moving your finger along the arrow. Then, have the students say the sentence in unison with you as you point again. Then have students say it without you. Continue by reading each sentence and then having the students repeat the sentence as you point to each word. Repeat the process with additional sentences. Then call on individual students to have them say the sentence as you point to the words. Remember that the purpose is to develop concepts of print; therefore, sentences should always be modeled for students before the student repeats the sentence. Although students will begin to recognize a few words during later lessons, the purpose is not word recognition but rather understanding what reading is all about (i.e., connecting print to meaningful oral language).

- Step 1: Read a sentence, pointing to each word and moving your finger along the arrow.
- Step 2: Have students say the sentence with you as you point to each word.
- Step 3: Have students say the sentence as you point to each word.
- Step 4: Read the next sentence as you point to each word.
- Step 5: Have students say the sentence as you point to each word.
- Step 6: Repeat steps 4 and 5 until all sentences have been completed.
- Step 7: Call on individual students to say at least one sentence as you point to each word.

IN THE REAL WORLD

Model reading the sentence as much as is necessary for students to be able to say the sentence on their own. Sentences gradually increase in length as the lessons progress. If students are unable to repeat an entire sentence, break the sentence into parts.

Questions and Answers

Lesson 94

Part B: Point and Read

(Hold up the book.) **Let's point and read. Look at this first sentence about the story we read in our last lesson. My turn. Watch my finger while I read the sentence.** *(Point to the word, moving your finger along the arrow.)* ***The kitten jumps on Ginger's back.***

Great. Now it's your turn. I'll point to the words. You say the sentence. *(Call on each student. Point to the word, moving your finger along the arrow.)* **The kitten jumps on Ginger's back.**

Repeat the process in Parts A and B by first blending the following words and then pointing at and reading those words in the sentences:
- **hid, bush** (sentence: **Ginger hid under a bush, and the girl found him.**)
- **two, cats, box** (sentence: **The two cats sleep in a box.**)

Maxwell is very impressed with your hard work! He and I will give you a check mark.

The kitten jumps on Ginger's back.

80 Lesson 94

Ginger hid under a bush,
and the girl found him.

The two cats sleep in
a box.

Strand Seven: Letter-Sound Correspondence

Students must learn letter-sound correspondences in order to be able to sound out words when reading. As discussed in the section titled The Phonology of English, the system of letter-sound correspondences for our language is complex. In order to keep letter-sound correspondence as simple and clear as possible for the students, letter-sounds are taught one at a time throughout the curriculum. Once a new letter-sound is introduced, students have opportunities to practice associating the sound with the letter repeatedly before another letter-sound is introduced. Additionally, once students have learned a letter-sound, review of that letter-sound is provided throughout the rest of the curriculum.

Letter-Sound Introduction: Begins in Lesson 42 and ends in Lesson 116

In Letter-Sound Introduction, students are taught the sound for a letter whose name they already know. First, show the students the letter-sound card and remind them of the name of the letter. Then tell them the letter's sound. Have students say the sound with you. Then have them say the sound without you. Tell students that both the big ways and the little ways to write the letter make the same sound. Provide individual practice saying the sound for both the big letter and the little letter. Next, read the poem for that letter-sound, emphasizing the words that begin with the sound they are learning. When the sound is a continuous sound, hold the sound for two or three seconds each time. After reading the poem, show the letter-sound card again and remind students again of the letter-sound.

ACTIVITY AT A GLANCE

- Step 1: Show the letter-sound card to the students. Remind them of the letter name, and tell them the letter-sound.
- Step 2: Have students say the letter-sound with you.
- Step 3: Have students say the letter-sound without you.
- Step 4: Tell students that both the big ways and the little ways to write the letter make the same sound.
- Step 5: Provide individual practice saying the sound for both the big letter and the little letter.
- Step 6: Read the poem, emphasizing words that begin with the letter-sound and holding continuous sounds for 2 or 3 seconds.
- Step 7: Show the letter-sound card again, and remind students again of the letter-sound.

IN THE REAL WORLD

For students with intellectual disabilities, provide a magnet letter. Touch the letter and say the letter-sound. Have the student touch the letter and say the sound with you. Once the student can do it with you, have the student do it without you.

Questions and Answers

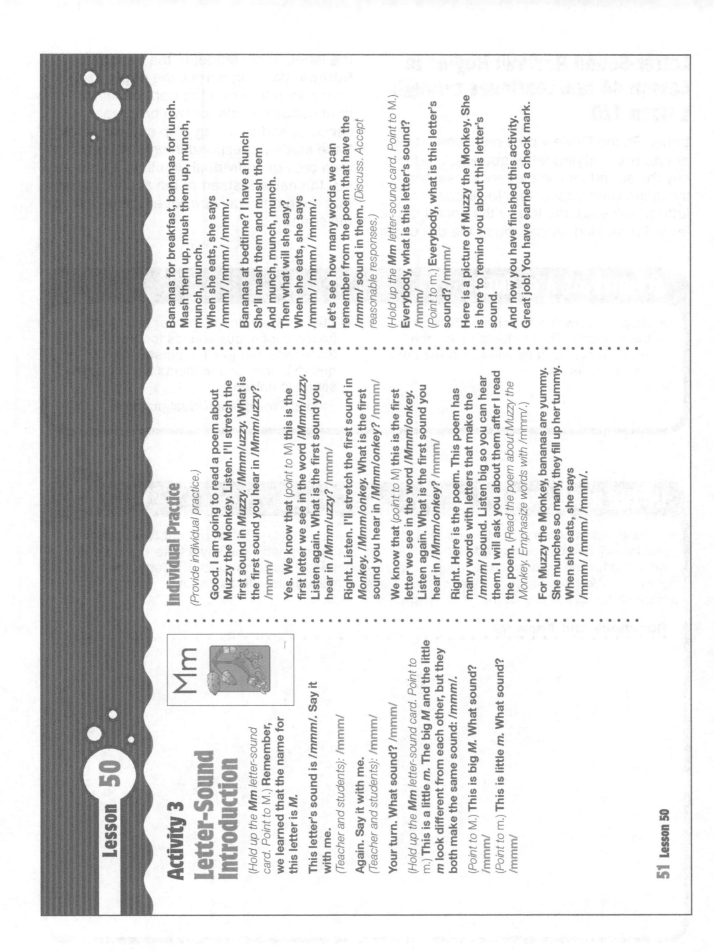

Lesson 50

Activity 3
Letter-Sound Introduction

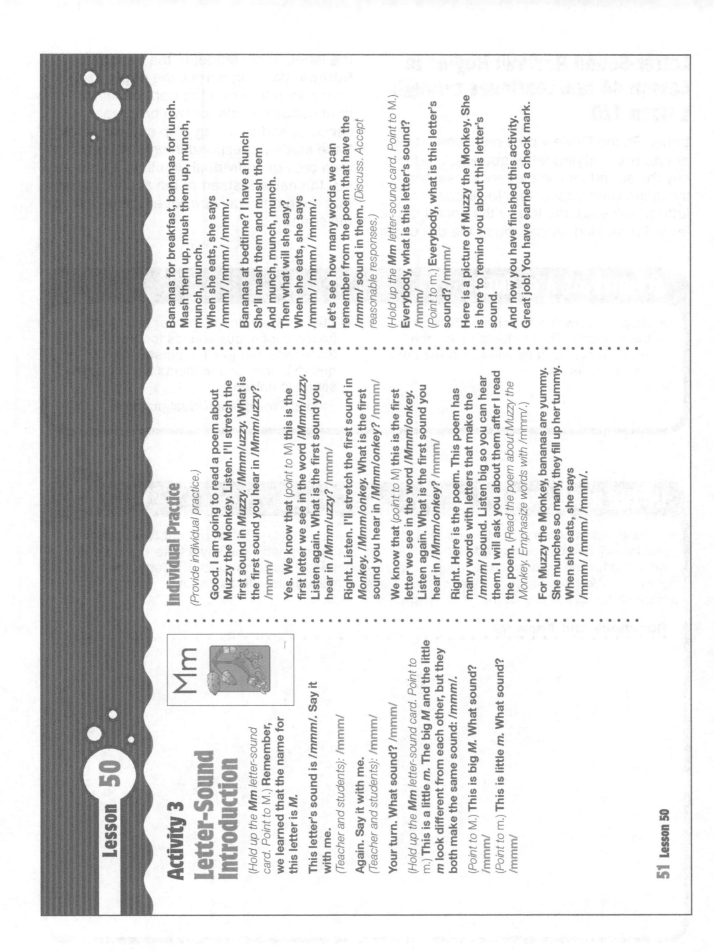

Mm

(Hold up the Mm letter-sound card. Point to M.) **Remember, we learned that the name for this letter is M.**

This letter's sound is /mmm/. Say it with me.
(Teacher and students): /mmm/

Again. Say it with me.
(Teacher and students): /mmm/

Your turn. What sound? /mmm/

(Hold up the Mm letter-sound card. Point to m.) **This is a little m. The big M and the little m look different from each other, but they both make the same sound:** /mmm/.

(Point to M.) **This is big M. What sound?** /mmm/
(Point to m.) **This is little m. What sound?** /mmm/

Individual Practice

(Provide individual practice.)

Good. I am going to read a poem about Muzzy the Monkey. Listen. I'll stretch the first sound in Muzzy. /Mmm/uzzy. What is the first sound you hear in /Mmm/uzzy? /mmm/

Yes. We know that *(point to M)* **this is the first letter we see in the word /Mmm/uzzy. Listen again. What is the first sound you hear in /Mmm/uzzy?** /mmm/

Right. Listen. I'll stretch the first sound in Monkey. /Mmm/onkey. What is the first sound you hear in /Mmm/onkey? /mmm/

We know that *(point to M)* **this is the first letter we see in the word /Mmm/onkey. Listen again. What is the first sound you hear in /Mmm/onkey?** /mmm/

Right. Here is the poem. This poem has many words with letters that make the /mmm/ sound. Listen big so you can hear them. I will ask you about them after I read the poem. *(Read the poem about Muzzy the Monkey. Emphasize words with /mmm/.)*

For Muzzy the Monkey, bananas are yummy. She munches so many, they fill up her tummy. When she eats, she says /mmm/ /mmm/ /mmm/.

Bananas for breakfast, bananas for lunch. Mash them up, mush them up, munch, munch, munch. When she eats, she says /mmm/ /mmm/ /mmm/.

Bananas at bedtime? I have a hunch She'll mash them and mush them And munch, munch, munch. Then what will she say? When she eats, she says /mmm/ /mmm/ /mmm/.

Let's see how many words we can remember from the poem that have the /mmm/ sound in them. *(Discuss. Accept reasonable responses.)*

(Hold up the Mm letter-sound card. Point to M.) **Everybody, what is this letter's sound?** /mmm/

(Point to m.) **Everybody, what is this letter's sound?** /mmm/

Here is a picture of Muzzy the Monkey. She is here to remind you about this letter's sound.

And now you have finished this activity. Great job! You have earned a check mark.

Letter-Sound Review: Begins in Lesson 44 and continues through Lesson 120

Letter-Sound Review provides cumulative practice identifying letter-sounds. Students say the sounds for the letters presented, including both capital and lowercase letters. Tell students to say the sound of the letter for as long as you touch the dot under the letter. Show students the **Teacher's Edition.** Working across the page, touch under each letter on the dot, touching continuous sounds for two or three seconds and touching stop sounds quickly. Have students respond in unison first, and then provide individual practice. If students say the name instead of the sound, confirm that the name was correct and then ask for the sound.

ACTIVITY AT A GLANCE

- Step 1: Show the **Teacher's Edition** to the students. Tell students to say the sound for as long as you touch the dot under the letter.

- Step 2: Touch the dot under each letter (touch continuous sounds for 2 or 3 seconds and touch stop sounds quickly), and have students say the letter-sound in unison.
- Step 3: Provide individual practice.

IN THE REAL WORLD

To modify this activity for students with intellectual disabilities, provide letter magnets for the letter-sounds being reviewed. You can touch the letter and have students say the sound. If students still struggle, you can put out two different letter magnets. You say a letter-sound and have the students touch the letter that corresponds with that sound.

Questions and Answers

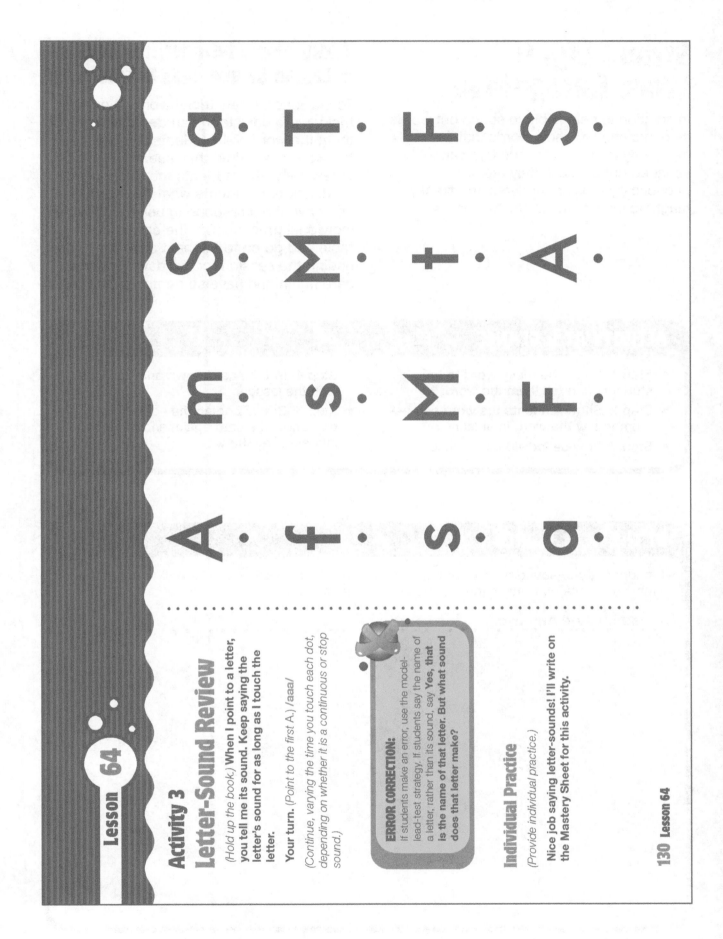

A · m · S · q ·

f · s · M · T ·

s · M · t · F ·

q · F · A · S ·

Activity 3
Letter-Sound Review

(Hold up the book.) **When I point to a letter, you tell me its sound. Keep saying the letter's sound for as long as I touch the letter.**

Your turn. *(Point to the first A.)* /aaa/

(Continue, varying the time you touch each dot, depending on whether it is a continuous or stop sound.)

ERROR CORRECTION:
If students make an error, use the model-lead-test strategy. If students say the name of a letter, rather than its sound, say **Yes, that is the name of that letter. But what sound does that letter make?**

Individual Practice

(Provide individual practice.)

Nice job saying letter-sounds! I'll write on the Mastery Sheet for this activity.

130 Lesson 64

Strand Eight: Word Recognition

In addition to being able to sound out words, students need to know words that appear frequently in children's texts that cannot be sounded out because they are not phonetically regular. Students are directly taught to identify these "tricky" words.

Tricky Words Introduction: Begins in Lesson 82 and ends in Lesson 114

To introduce a new tricky word, show the tricky word card to the students and tell them the word. Tell students they will say the word every time they see it. Several times, show the students the tricky word card, ask the students what the word is, and have them respond in unison. Provide individual practice. Set the card on the table and go on to the next activity. Before ending the session for the day, show the card again and have students say the word.

ACTIVITY AT A GLANCE

- Step 1: Show the tricky word to the students and tell them the word.
- Step 2: Show students the word and ask them to say the word in unison.
- Step 3: Provide individual practice.
- Step 4: Put the card down and continue with the lesson.
- Step 5: Before ending the session for the day, show the card again, and have the students say the word.

IN THE REAL WORLD

If students try to sound out the word, remind students that they cannot sound out this word because the letters do not make their sounds the right way.

Questions and Answers

Tricky Words Review: Begins in Lesson 84 and ends in Lesson 120

Students will learn to automatically recognize tricky words by having repeated practice recognizing these words. To review previously taught tricky words, show students one tricky word card at a time and have the students read each card in unison. Mix up the cards and have the students read them again. Provide individual practice reading the words.

ACTIVITY AT A GLANCE

- Step 1: Show students one tricky word card at a time and have the students read each card in unison.

- Step 2: Mix up the cards and have the students read them again.
- Step 3: Provide individual practice reading the words.

IN THE REAL WORLD

If students try to sound out the word, remind students that they cannot sound out this word because the letters do not make their sounds the right way.

Questions and Answers

Activity 3
Tricky Words

Part A: New

(Have ready Tricky Word Cards 1–5.)

Now we are going to learn a new tricky word.

(Hold up Tricky Word Card 5—he.) **This word is he. What is this word?** he
Every time you see this word, what will you say? he

(Put the new word into the deck with the rest of the tricky words.)

Part B: Review

Now it's time to review the rest of our tricky words.

(Hold up Tricky Word Card 3—a.) **Everybody, what is this word?** a

> **Repeat the process with Tricky Word Cards 1, 2, 4, and 5.**

Individual Practice

(Shuffle the tricky word cards, and ask students to say each word again in unison. Then have each student say each word individually.)

Nice work with tricky words! I'll give you a check mark.

69 Lesson 92

Sample Lessons

Here are three sample lessons, one from each **Teacher's Edition.** These lessons show how the skills integrate and develop throughout the curriculum.

(Review rules quickly.)

Sit tall.
Listen big.
Answer when I cue.
Answer together.

Activity 1
Picture Naming

We are going to look at some pictures and then name them. *(Hold up the book, and point to the pictures.)* **The names of the pictures are *mail, rain, feet, shell, moon, fish.***

Now say all the names of the pictures as I point to them. *(Quickly point to each picture.)* mail, rain, feet, shell, moon, fish

Individual Practice
(Provide individual practice.)

Great job! I will check the Mastery Sheet, and we can continue.

Activity 2
First-Sound Pictures

Stretching

(Have ready Picture Magnets 2, 17, 18, 20, and 21.)

Now we are going to think about the first sound in each word. *(Place Picture Magnets 20 and 21 on the marker board.)*

(Point to Picture Magnet 20.) **This is shell.** *(Point to Picture Magnet 21.)* **This is moon. Listen. /Mmm/. Which of the things in these pictures begins with /mmm/?** moon

Right. Moon begins with /mmm/.

ERROR CORRECTION:
If students make an error, use the model-lead-test strategy.

Note: Make sure students stretch continuous sounds for 2 to 3 seconds.

Repeat the process with the following:
- **Picture Magnets 18 and 2**
- **Picture Magnets 2 and 17**

Individual Practice

(Provide individual practice.)

You did a great job listening for the sound at the beginning of the word! I'll give you a check mark for this activity.

Activity 3
First-Sound Game

Now we are going to do something different. We are going to think about the first sound in a word, but we won't be using pictures. This is called the First-Sound Game. I'll say a word. When I cue, tell me the first sound you hear in the word. *(Demonstrate holding up one finger.)* **I'll do one first.**

My turn. Shell. What is the first sound in shell? *(Hold up one finger.)* **/Sh/. Do you hear it? Shell.** *(Pause.)* **/Sh/.**

Listen for the first sound. Do it with me. Shell. *(Pause.)* **What's the first sound you hear?**
(Teacher and students:) **/sh/**
Yes, the first sound we hear in shell is /sh/.

Now it's your turn. I'll say a word. When I cue, you tell me the first sound you hear in the word. Remember to answer together on my cue.

First word. *Fish.* (Pause.) **What is the first sound in *fish*?** /fff/ (Hold up one finger.) /fff/. **Very good. The first sound in *fish* is /fff/.**

New word. *Feet.* **What is the first sound in *feet*?** (Hold up one finger.) /fff/

Next word.

Note: Make sure students stretch continuous sounds for 2 to 3 seconds.

Repeat the process with the following words: /mmm/ail, /mmm/oon, /rrr/ain.

Individual Practice

(Provide individual practice.)

We have finished this part of our lesson. I will make a check mark for this activity. You did a great job!

Activity 4
Oral Blending
Say-the-Word Game

(Use Maxwell the puppet to speak words in stretched form.)

Now we are going to play Say the Word. Remember, Maxwell can say words only in a funny way. Whenever he says a word, it is stretched. You have to tell me what word he said the fast way. I will do the first one.

Maxwell, first word.

(Speaking through Maxwell:) /Fff/eet. (Use the hand cues for stretching.) **What word did Maxwell say?** feet

Yes, feet.

Repeat the process with the following words: /sh/ell, /mmm/oon, /rrr/ain, /mmm/ail, /fff/ish.

(Scaffold as necessary.)

Individual Practice

(Provide individual practice.)

Great job! Let's make a check mark on the Mastery Sheet.

Lesson 10

Activity 5
Part A: Letter Introduction

(Hold up the **Mm** letter-sound card. Cover the lowercase m at the top of the card with a sticky note.)

(Point to the monkey.) **Here is a picture of Muzzy Monkey. His name has two M's in it.** (Point to M.) **This letter is M. Say it with me when I touch it.** (Call on students.)

(Teacher and students:) M
Again. Say it with me.
(Teacher and students:) M

(Point to M.) **We are going to learn the name of the letter M. What is this letter? Say its name together when I touch it.** (Cue.) M
Again. Say it together. (Cue.) M

Individual Practice

(Provide individual practice.)

(Hold up the book. Point to Muzzy Monkey.)

This says Muzzy Monkey. (Point to the M in Muzzy.) **Muzzy begins with this letter. What letter? M**

(Point to the M in Monkey.) **What is this letter? M**
What letter is at the beginning of Muzzy? M
What letter is at the beginning of Monkey? M

(Provide individual practice. Scaffold if necessary. Circle the M's, if needed.)

Muzzy Monkey

40 Lesson 10

M t O T M

t O t O T

Part B: Letter Review

(Hold up the book.) **Let's practice letter names we have learned. When I point to a letter, say its name.**

(Point to M.) **M**

(Point to each letter, remembering to move from left to right across the page.)

ERROR CORRECTION:
My Turn *(Say letter name.)*
Together *(Say letter name with students.)*
Your Turn *(Students say letter name.)*
(Back up 2 items and continue.)

Individual Practice

(Provide individual practice.)

You are doing a great job of listening big, sitting tall, and answering together. Let's move on!

41 Lesson 10

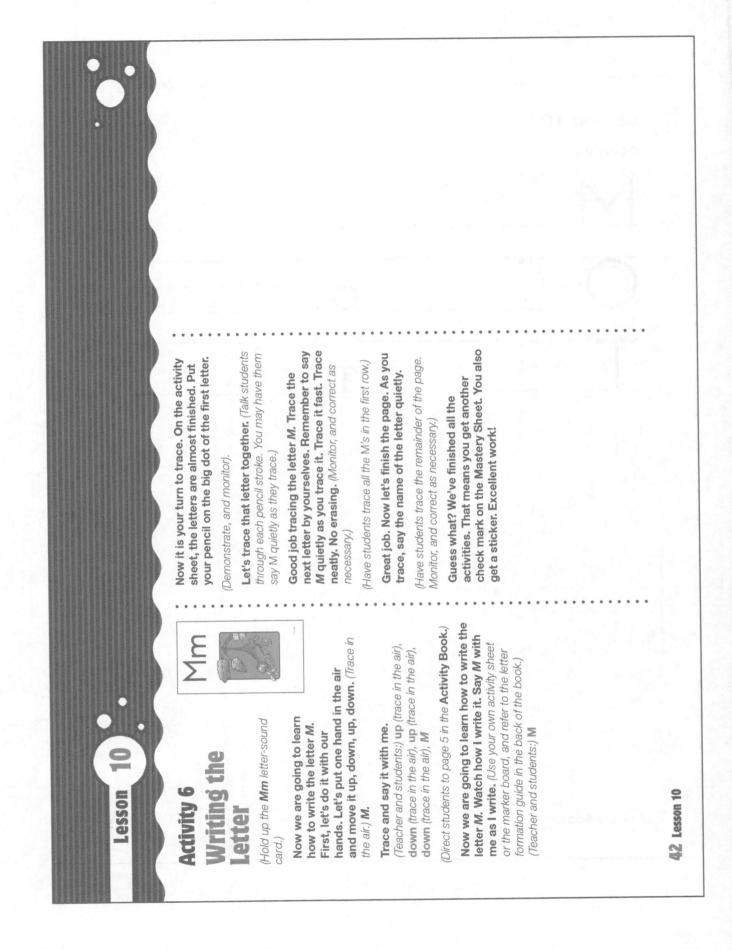

Lesson 10

Activity 6
Writing the Letter

(Hold up the Mm letter-sound card.)

Now we are going to learn how to write the letter *M*. First, let's do it with our hands. Let's put one hand in the air and move it up, down, up, down. *(Trace in the air.)* ***M***.

Trace and say it with me. *(Teacher and students:)* **up** *(trace in the air)*, **down** *(trace in the air)*, **up** *(trace in the air)*, **down** *(trace in the air)*, ***M***

(Direct students to page 5 in the Activity Book.)

Now we are going to learn how to write the letter *M*. Watch how I write it. Say *M* with me as I write. *(Use your own activity sheet or the marker board, and refer to the letter formation guide in the back of the book.)* *(Teacher and students:)* **M**

Now it is your turn to trace. On the activity sheet, the letters are almost finished. Put your pencil on the big dot of the first letter.

(Demonstrate, and monitor).

Let's trace that letter together. *(Talk students through each pencil stroke. You may have them say M quietly as they trace.)*

Good job tracing the letter *M*. Trace the next letter by yourselves. Remember to say *M* quietly as you trace it. Trace it fast. Trace neatly. No erasing. *(Monitor, and correct as necessary.)*

(Have students trace all the M's in the first row.)

Great job. Now let's finish the page. As you trace, say the name of the letter quietly.

(Have students trace the remainder of the page. Monitor, and correct as necessary.)

Guess what? We've finished all the activities. That means you get another check mark on the Mastery Sheet. You also get a sticker. Excellent work!

42 Lesson 10

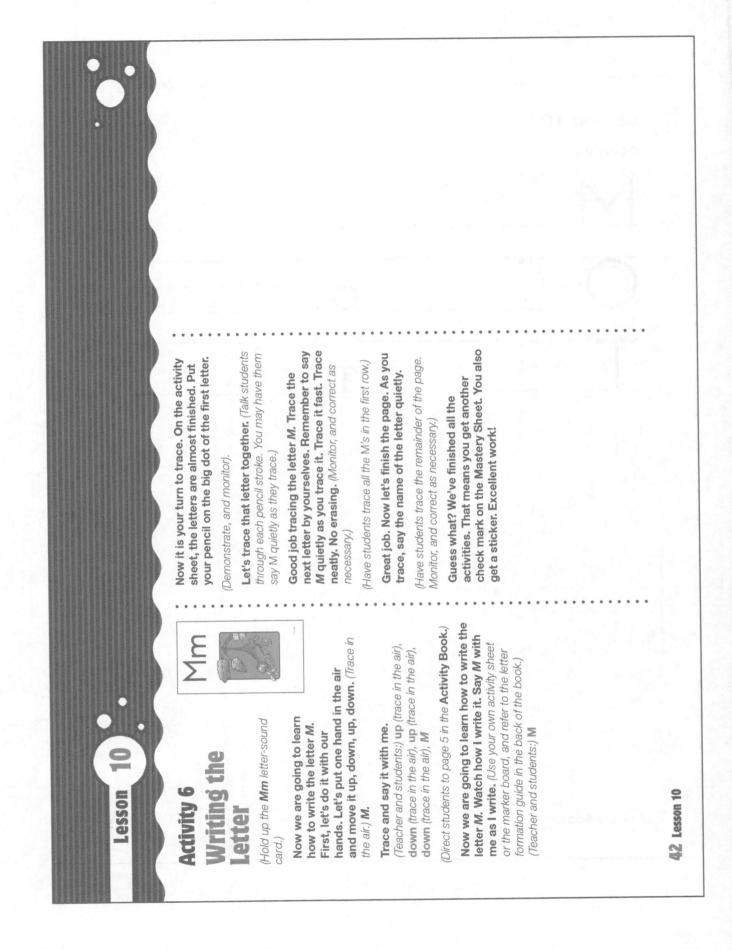

Name

Lesson 10

Activity 6

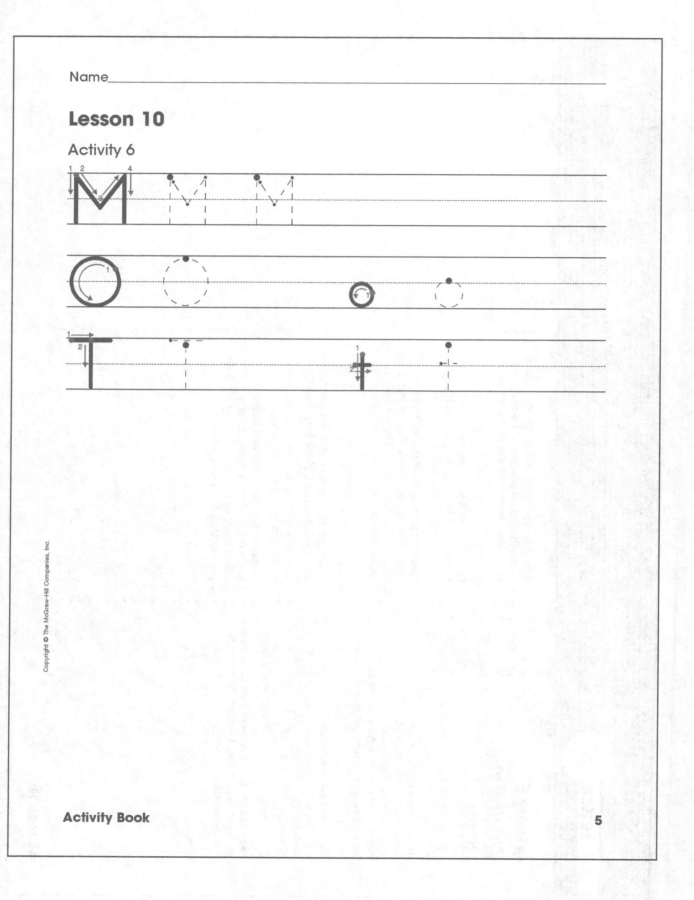

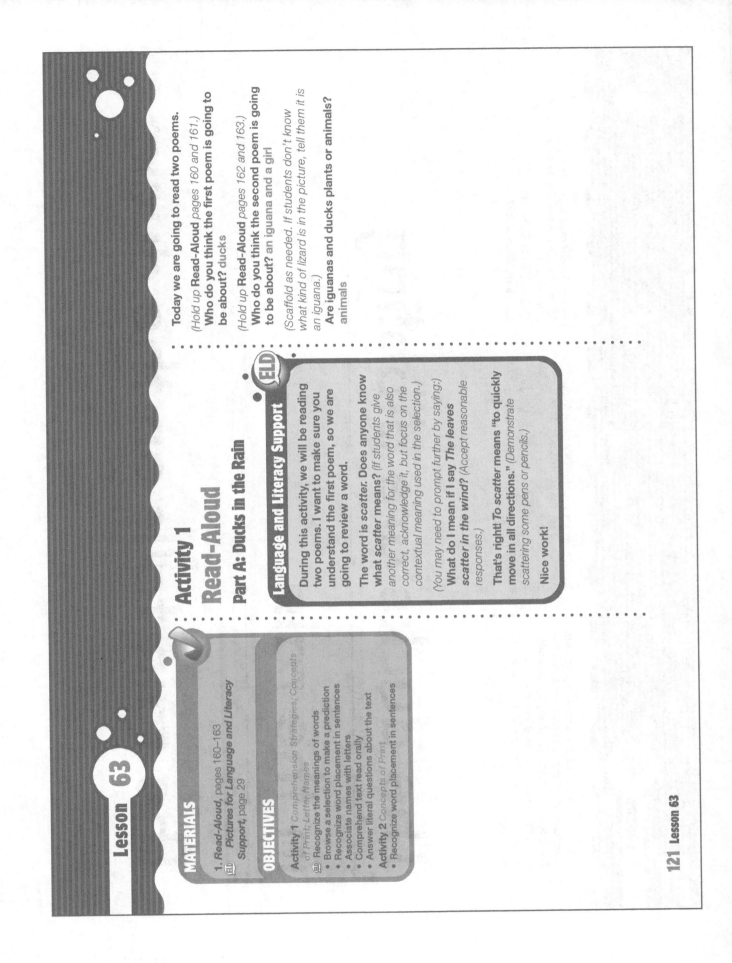

Lesson 63

MATERIALS

1. *Read-Aloud*, pages 160–163
   (ELD) *Pictures for Language and Literacy Support*, page 29

OBJECTIVES

Activity 1 *Comprehension Strategies; Concepts of Print; Letter Names*
(ELD)
• Recognize the meanings of words
• Browse a selection to make a prediction
• Recognize word placement in sentences
• Associate names with letters
• Comprehend text read orally
• Answer literal questions about the text

Activity 2 *Concepts of Print*
• Recognize word placement in sentences

Today we are going to read two poems.

(Hold up Read-Aloud pages 160 and 161.)
Who do you think the first poem is going to be about? ducks

(Hold up Read-Aloud pages 162 and 163.)
Who do you think the second poem is going to be about? an iguana and a girl

(Scaffold as needed. If students don't know what kind of lizard is in the picture, tell them it is an iguana.)
Are iguanas and ducks plants or animals? animals

Activity 1
Read-Aloud
Part A: Ducks in the Rain

(ELD)

Language and Literacy Support

During this activity, we will be reading two poems. I want to make sure you understand the first poem, so we are going to review a word.

The word is *scatter*. Does anyone know what *scatter* means? *(If students give another meaning for the word that is also correct, acknowledge it, but focus on the contextual meaning used in the selection.)*

(You may need to prompt further by saying:)
What do I mean if I say *The leaves scatter in the wind*? *(Accept reasonable responses.)*

That's right! *To scatter* means "to quickly move in all directions." *(Demonstrate scattering some pens or pencils.)*

Nice work!

(Hold up the book.) **Now it's time to point and read. Let's look at two sentences about the first poem. My turn. Watch my finger while I read the first sentence.** *(Point to each word, moving your finger along the arrow.)* ***The ducks are dibbling in the rain.***

Great. Now it's your turn. I'll point to the words. You say the sentence. *(Call on each student. Point to each word, moving your finger along the arrow.)* **The ducks are dibbling in the rain.**

(Hold up **Read-Aloud** *page 160. Point to d.)* **Remember, this is the little letter d. Say d with me.**
(Teacher and students:) **d**
Your turn. What letter? d

The ducks are dibbling
in the rain.

The rain falls on the ducks.

(Hold up the book.) **How many little *d*'s are in this first sentence?** (Call on students.) two (Scaffold as needed.)

Right. There are two little *d*'s in this first sentence.

(Hold up the book.) **Let's look at the second sentence. My turn. Watch my finger while I read the second sentence.** (Point to each word, moving your finger along the arrow.) **The rain falls on the ducks.**

Great. Now it's your turn. I'll point to the words. You say the sentence. (Call on each student. Point to each word, moving your finger along the arrow.) **The rain falls on the ducks.**

How many little *d*'s are in this second sentence? (Call on students.) one (Scaffold as needed.)

Right. There is one little *d* in this second sentence.

(Hold up Read-Aloud page 160. Point to the title.) **Watch my finger while I read the title of this poem.** (Point to each word.) ***Ducks in the Rain***

Great. Now it's your turn. I'll point to the words. You say the title of the poem. (Call on each student. Point to each word.) Ducks in the Rain

Let's read the poem now. Listen to find out what happens to the ducks. (While holding the book for students to see, read aloud page 160.)

Good listening. Now let's review what we learned in our book.

What are the ducks doing? dibbling and dabbling in the rain

What do you think it means to dibble and dabble? (Accept reasonable responses, such as to play in or with something.)

Do you think you would like to play with ducks in the rain? Why or why not? (Answers will vary.)

ERROR CORRECTION:
If students speak in short sentences or do not speak in complete sentences, expand on their language by telling them a sentence that uses as many of their words as possible. Then have the student repeat the sentence. If students are highly engaged, spend a few minutes modeling longer sentences and having students repeat the sentences.

Part B: Lizard Longing

Language and Literacy Support

I want to make sure you understand the next poem, so we are going to review some words.

The first word is scaly. Who knows what scaly means? (If students give another meaning, acknowledge it, but focus on the meaning used in the selection.)

(You may need to prompt further by saying:) **What do I mean if I say *The fish felt scaly in my hand*?** (Accept reasonable responses.)

Yes! If something is scaly, that means it is hard and rough. (If you have something scaly in the classroom, allow students to feel it.)

The last word is *piranha*. Does anyone know what a piranha is? (If students give another meaning, acknowledge it, but focus on the meaning used in the selection.)

(You may need to prompt further by saying:) **What do I mean if I say *A piranha has very sharp teeth*?** (Accept reasonable responses.)

That's right! A piranha is a dangerous fish. (Hold up Pictures for Language and Literacy Support page 29.)

Great job!

(Hold up Read-Aloud pages 162 and 163.) **How do you think the girl and the iguana feel in this picture? Why?** *(Accept reasonable responses, such as* The girl and the iguana look happy and probably like being together. *Scaffold as needed.)*

(Hold up the book.) **Now it's time to point and read. Let's look at two sentences about the second poem. My turn. Watch my finger while I read the first sentence.** *(Point to each word, moving your finger along the arrow.)* ***I'm gonna tell Mama I want an iguana.***

Great. Now it's your turn. I'll point to the words. You say the sentence. *(Point to each word, moving your finger along the arrow.)* I'm gonna tell Mama I want an iguana.

(Hold up the book.) **How many big *I*'s are in this first sentence?** *(Call on students.)* two *(Scaffold as needed.)* **Right. There are two big *I*'s in this first sentence.**

How many little *i*'s are in this first sentence? *(Call on students.)* one *(Scaffold as needed.)* **Right. There is one little *i* in this first sentence.**

I'm gonna tell Mama I want an iguana.

I wish I had an iguana.

Lesson 63

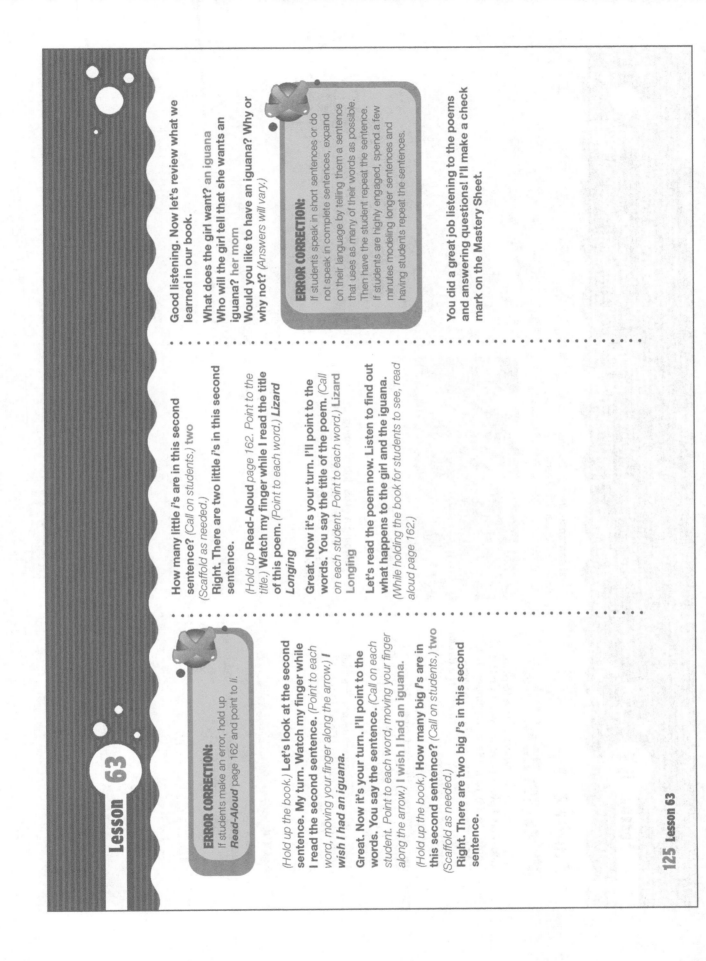

ERROR CORRECTION:
If students make an error, hold up *Read-Aloud* page 162 and point to *Ii*.

(Hold up the book.) **Let's look at the second sentence. My turn. Watch my finger while I read the second sentence.** *(Point to each word, moving your finger along the arrow.)* **I wish I had an iguana.**

Great. Now it's your turn. I'll point to the words. You say the sentence. *(Call on each student. Point to each word, moving your finger along the arrow.)* **I wish I had an iguana.**

(Hold up the book.) **How many big I's are in this second sentence?** *(Call on students.)* two *(Scaffold as needed.)*
Right. There are two big I's in this second sentence.

How many little i's are in this second sentence? *(Call on students.)* two *(Scaffold as needed.)*
Right. There are two little i's in this second sentence.

(Hold up Read-Aloud page 162. Point to the title.) **Watch my finger while I read the title of this poem.** *(Point to each word.)* ***Lizard Longing***

Great. Now it's your turn. I'll point to the words. You say the title of the poem. *(Call on each student. Point to each word.)* ***Lizard Longing***

Let's read the poem now. Listen to find out what happens to the girl and the iguana. *(While holding the book for students to see, read aloud page 162.)*

Good listening. Now let's review what we learned in our book.

What does the girl want? an iguana
Who will the girl tell that she wants an iguana? her mom
Would you like to have an iguana? Why or why not? *(Answers will vary.)*

ERROR CORRECTION:
If students speak in short sentences or do not speak in complete sentences, expand on their language by telling them a sentence that uses as many of their words as possible. Then have the student repeat the sentence. If students are highly engaged, spend a few minutes modeling longer sentences and having students repeat the sentences.

You did a great job listening to the poems and answering questions! I'll make a check mark on the Mastery Sheet.

125 Lesson 63

Lesson 63

Activity 2
Point and Read

(Hold up the book.) **Now it's time to point and read. Let's look at the words in this sentence. My turn. Watch my finger while I read the sentence.** *(Point to each word, moving your finger along the arrow.)* **The ducks are dibbling in the rain.**

Great. Now it's your turn. I'll point to the words. You say the sentence. *(Call on each student. Point to each word, moving your finger along the arrow.)* **The ducks are dibbling in the rain.**

Very good! Here's a picture of what that sentence says. *(Hold up Read-Aloud pages 160 and 161.)*

Next sentence. *(Remember, students are expected to repeat the sentence but not to recognize each printed word individually.)*

Repeat the process with the following sentences:
- **The rain falls on the ducks.** (pages 160 and 161)
- **I'm gonna tell Mama I want an iguana.** (pages 162 and 163)
- **I like iguanas.** (pages 162 and 163)

Individual Practice

(Provide individual practice.)

You're doing a great job pointing and reading, and you have finished both this activity and the lesson. What should I do now?

The ducks are dibbling

in the rain.

The rain falls on the ducks.

I'm gonna tell Mama I

want an iguana.

I like iguanas.

Lesson 63

128 Lesson 63

110

Staff Development Guide, Level K

Lesson 100

MATERIALS

1. Maxwell
2. Tricky Words Cards 1–6
3. *Activity Book*, page 50
4. *Stop-and-Go Game* (Yellow Level)
5. Assessment 5

OBJECTIVES

Activity 1 *Phonemic Awareness; Concepts of Print*
- Blend phonemes to say words
- Recognize word placement in sentences

Activity 2 *Phonemic Awareness*
- Segment spoken words into sounds
- Understand that each finger represents one sound in a word

Activity 3 *Word Recognition and Spelling*
- Learn to automatically recognize irregular words

Activity 4 *Letter-Sound Correspondences*
- Associate sounds with letters

Activity 5 *Letter Names*
- Associate names with letters

Activity 6 *Letter Names*
- Identify and write letters

Activity 7 *Phonemic Awareness*
- Blend phonemes to say words
- Segment spoken words into sounds

Activity 1
Oral Blending

Part A: Say-the-Word Game

Let's listen to Maxwell say words that are about the story we read in the last lesson. When Maxwell says a word, he will say the whole word slowly so you can hear every sound.

(Maxwell:) /Mmm/ /ī/ /sss/.
What word? mice
Yes, *mice.*

Repeat the process with the following words: **taste, cheese.**

ERROR CORRECTION:
If students make an error, gradually shorten the length of the first sound.

Individual Practice

(Provide individual practice with 1 or 2 words per student.)

Part B: Point and Read

(Hold up the next page of the book.) Now it's time to point and read. Let's look at this first sentence about the story we read yesterday. **My turn. Watch my finger while I read the sentence.** *(Point to the word, moving your finger along the arrow.)* **Mice like to taste more than cheese.**

Great. Now it's your turn. I'll point to the words. You say the sentence. *(Call on each student. Point to the word, moving your finger along the arrow.)* Mice like to taste more than cheese.

Repeat the process in Parts A and B by first blending the following words and then pointing at and reading those words in the sentences:

- **mouse, ate, hole** (sentence: The mouse ate a hole in my blanket.)
- **toast** (sentence: The mouse ate a hole in my toast.)
- **holes, cake** (sentence: The mouse ate holes in my cake and my basket.)

You are all listening very well. You get a check mark.

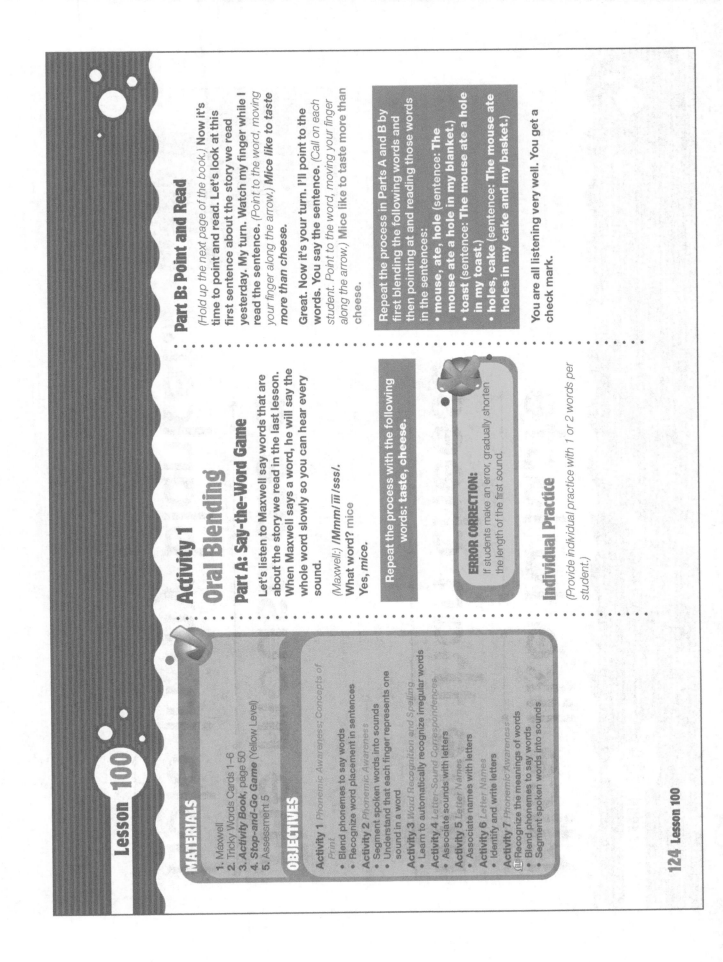

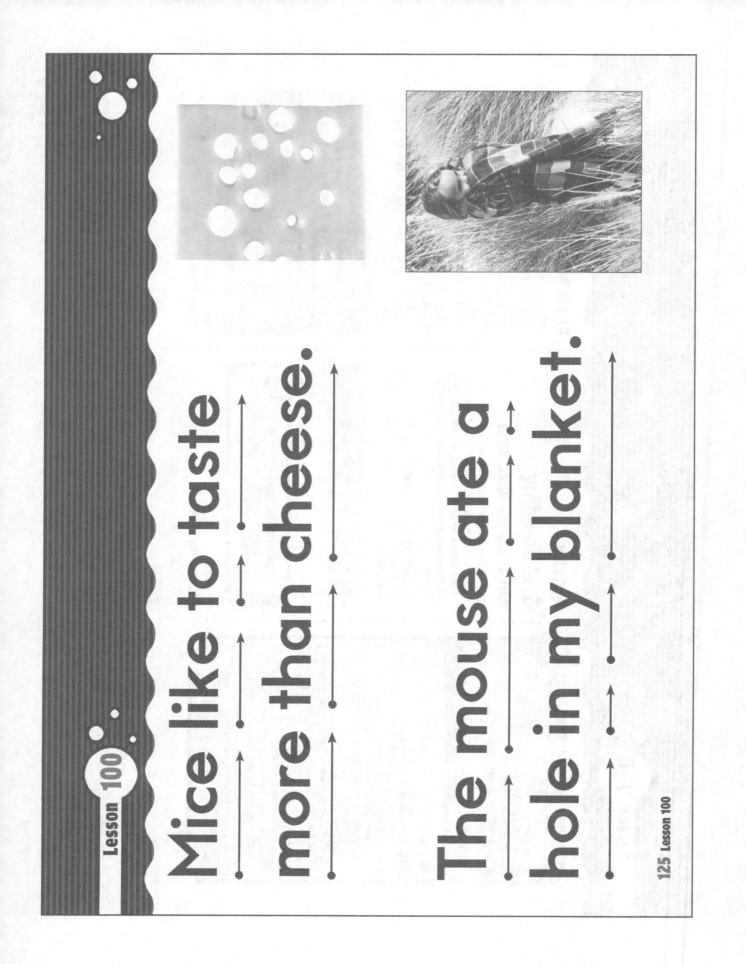

Mice like to taste
more than cheese.

The mouse ate a
hole in my blanket.

125 Lesson 100

112   Staff Development Guide, Level K

The mouse ate a hole in my toast.

The mouse ate holes in my cake and my basket.

Staff Development Guide, Level K

Activity 2
Stretch-the-Word Game

Listen to this sentence about the story we read in the last lesson. *Mice like to taste more than cheese.*

Now you are going to play Stretch the Word. When we stretch the word, we say each sound slowly.

Fists up. *(Pause.) Mice. (Pause.) Stretch mice.* /mmm/ /īīī/ /sss/

Repeat the process with the following words: **taste, cheese.**

ERROR CORRECTION:
If students make an error, use the model-lead-test strategy.

Listen to the sentence again. *Mice like to taste more than cheese.*

Next sentence.

Repeat the process by first reading the following sentences and then stretching the words:
• **The mouse ate a hole in my blanket.** (words: mouse, ate, hole)
• **The mouse ate a hole in my toast.** (word: toast)
• **The mouse ate holes in my cake and my basket.** (words: holes, cake)

Individual Practice

(Provide individual practice with 1 or 2 words per student, but do not provide individual practice with the sentences.)

You are stretching words excellently. I'll give you a check mark!

Activity 3
Tricky Words

Part A: New

(Have ready Tricky Word Cards 1–6.)

Now we are going to learn a new tricky word.

(Hold up Tricky Word Card 6 — she.) **This word is *she*. What is this word?** *she*
Every time you see this word, what will you say? *she*

(Put the new word into the deck with the rest of the tricky words.)

Part B: Review

Now it's time to review the rest of our tricky words.

(Hold up Tricky Word Card 5 — he.) **Everybody, what is this word?** *he*

Repeat the process with Tricky Word Cards 1–4 and 6.

Individual Practice

(Shuffle the tricky word cards, and ask students to say each word again in unison. Then have each student say each word individually.)

Nice work with tricky words! I'll give you a check mark.

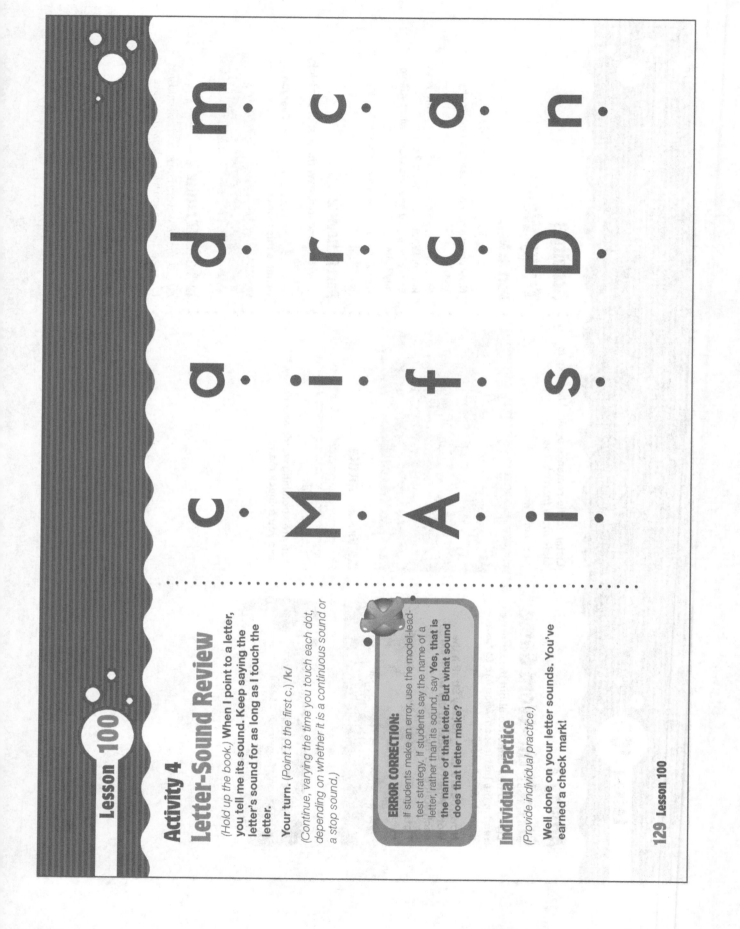

Lesson 100

c · a · d · m ·

M · i · r · c ·

A · f · c · a ·

i · s · D · n ·

Activity 4
Letter-Sound Review

(Hold up the book.) **When I point to a letter, you tell me its sound. Keep saying the letter's sound for as long as I touch the letter.**

Your turn. *(Point to the first c.)* /k/

(Continue, varying the time you touch each dot, depending on whether it is a continuous sound or a stop sound.)

ERROR CORRECTION:
If students make an error, use the model-lead-test strategy. If students say the name of a letter, rather than its sound, say **Yes, that is the name of that letter. But what sound does that letter make?**

Individual Practice
(Provide individual practice.)

Well done on your letter sounds. You've earned a check mark!

129 Lesson 100

116   **Staff Development Guide,** Level K

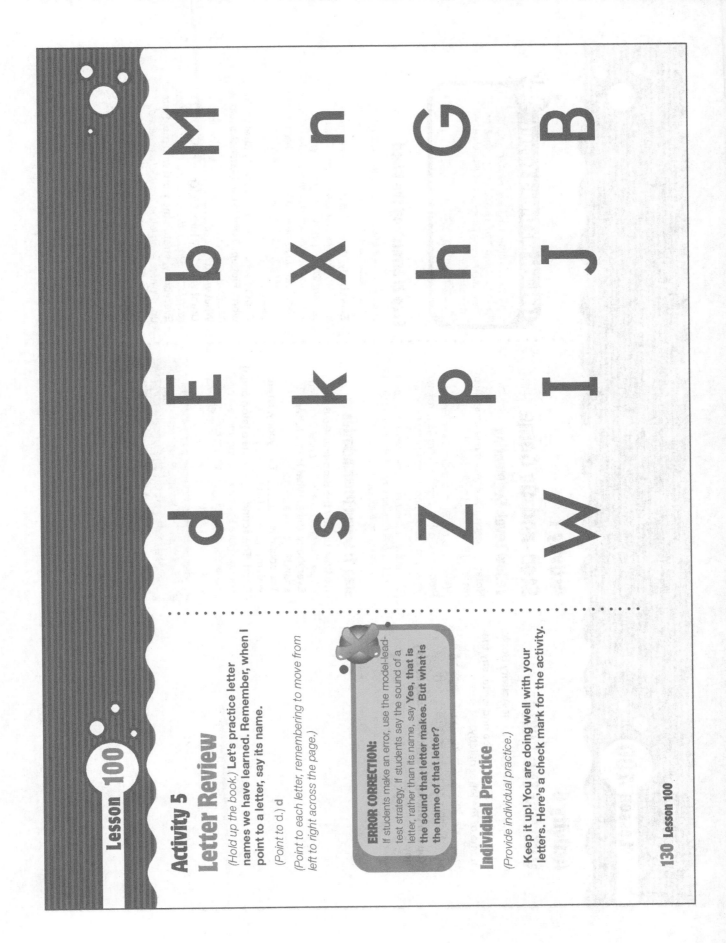

Lesson 100

Activity 5
Letter Review

(Hold up the book.) **Let's practice letter names we have learned. Remember, when I point to a letter, say its name.**

(Point to d.) d

(Point to each letter, remembering to move from left to right across the page.)

ERROR CORRECTION:
If students make an error, use the model-lead-test strategy. If students say the sound of a letter, rather than its name, say **Yes, that is the sound that letter makes. But what is the name of that letter?**

Individual Practice

(Provide individual practice.)

Keep it up! You are doing well with your letters. Here's a check mark for the activity.

130 Lesson 100

M b E d

n X k s

G h p Z

B J I W

Staff Development Guide, Level K

117

Activity 6
Writing the Letter

(Direct students to page 50 in the Activity Book.)

Remember, as you trace and write, say the name of the letter quietly.

(Have students trace and write the letters on the page. Monitor, and correct as necessary.)

You are writing so well! What should I do now?

Activity 7
Stop-and-Go Game

Yellow Level: Segmenting

Note: In Lesson 100, the game switches from blending to segmenting in Step 2.

(Have ready the Stop-and-Go Game Board, Stop-and-Go Mat, Build-a-Word Mat, Yellow Level letter cards, and game tokens.)

(Shuffle the Yellow Level letter cards and place them in a pile facedown near the game board. Divide the class into two teams.)

Step 1: Sound Pronunciation

It's time to play the Stop-and-Go Game! *(Draw and hold up a Yellow Level letter card.)* **Everybody, think. What is this letter's sound?** *(Call on a student.)*

The sound is _____. Everybody, say it with me. *(Scaffold as needed.)*

Good. The sound _____ is a [stop or go] sound. *(Have the same student move 1 or 2 spaces, depending on whether the sound is continuous or stop.)*

Repeat Step 1, calling on students from both teams, until there are enough letters to build one of the following words: fan, mad, and, man, sad, rat, ram, ran, tan, dad, am, Sam, at, fat, mat, sat.

Language and Literacy Support

If you build the word fan, mad, man, sad, rat, ram, ran, tan, dad, Sam, fat, mat, or sat, you may want to define the word, use the word in a sentence, or demonstrate the word meaning for students.

Step 2: Stretching the Word

(Once you have enough letters to build a word, ask for students' attention.)

Everybody, think. *(Call on the same student who identified the last letter-sound. Tell the student to build the word by moving those letters to spell the word on the Build-a-Word Mat. Scaffold as needed by saying each sound. Scaffold further as needed by pointing to the letters.)*

Good! *(Call on the same student.)* **Stretch this word. Fist up.** *(Point to each letter. Scaffold as needed.)*

What word? *(Scaffold as needed.)*

Great work! My turn. Listen to me. *(Point to each letter. Stretch the word and then say it fast.)* **Everybody, stretch the word with me. Fists up.** *(Point to each letter. Scaffold as needed.)* **Everybody, what word?** *(Say the word fast.)* **Yes!** *(Have the same student move 2 spaces.)*

131 Lesson 100

Lesson 100

Great work, everybody. Now I will draw another card.

Each time you complete Step 2, repeat Step 1 until a new word can be built. Draw cards, build and stretch words, and move tokens until one team reaches the stoplight at the end of the game board.

(Congratulate the team who won the game by moving the team's token to the stoplight.)

You are doing extremely well with the Stop-and-Go Game. Here's your check mark!

Before I give you a sticker for the lesson, however, let's review your tricky words.

(Shuffle Tricky Word Cards 1–6, and ask students to say each word in unison. Then have each student say each word individually.)

Nice job! Here's a sticker for the good work you've done on this lesson.

Student Assessment

(After completing Lesson 100, please turn to Assessment 5 in the **Placement and Assessment Guide.** *Administer the test to individual students.)*

TEACHER'S GUIDE

YELLOW LEVEL

Go Sounds	Stop Sounds
/nnn/	/d/
/rrr/	/t/
/aaa/	
/fff/	
/mmm/	
/sss/	

Word List

fan
mad
and
man
sad
rat
ram
ran
tan
dad
am
Sam
at
fat
mat
sat

132 Lesson 100

Lesson 100

Activity 6

X X   x x

B B   b b

D D   d d

P P   p p

G G   g g

50   **Activity Book**

Troubleshooting

Problem: Students do not respond on cue.

Solution: Remind students to answer together on cue. If the problem persists, discuss the importance of responding on cue. Remind students that answering together gives them all the opportunity to answer each question. Model the correct way to answer on cue, and practice it with your students. The best way to make sure students continue to answer on cue is to make sure they do it every time.

Problem: One student answers before the cue.

Solution: Validate the student for knowing the answer. Enlist the student to be your helper. Explain how helping means answering on cue. Review the importance of the group answering together. If a student seems to want individual attention, remind the student that everyone has the opportunity to answer by themselves during individual practice.

Problem: A student answers slightly behind the cue.

Solution: Praise the students who responded on cue. When a student answers slightly behind the cue, it usually means he or she does not really know the answer. Treat this as a normal error, and correct it with the Model-Lead-Test strategy. If a student consistently answers behind the cue, increase the think time between cues.

Problem: A student does not hold a continuous sound or mispronounces a sound.

Solution: Mispronouncing sounds causes problems for students when they are decoding and spelling words. Correct the mispronunciation with the Model-Lead-Test strategy. Model the correct way to say the sound. Have students say the sound in unison with you. Then have students say the sound without you. Back up two items and begin the task again.

Problem: One student in a group is having difficulty keeping up with the other students.

Solution: Provide a few minutes of one-on-one instruction. Integrate easier items into activities to ensure that the struggling student feels successful. If necessary, regroup the students.

Problem: A student refuses to work.

Solution: A student may be reluctant to work at first because he or she is unsure of what is expected, may not know the answer, or may be afraid to make a mistake. Create a positive, nurturing environment. Add external motivators such as stickers. Play the Beat the Teacher Game in which students get a point for every time they follow directions. However, if everyone in the group does not follow directions, you get a point.

Problem: You find yourself telling one student to sit up and another student to listen.

Solution: Reestablish rules. Examine your pacing. You may be too slow or inconsistent.

Glossary

Alphabetic Pertaining to a writing system that uses a symbol for each speech sound of the language. Of, relating to, or expressed by an alphabet.

Alphabetic Principle Use of letters and letter combinations to represent phonemes in an orthography. Refers to the fact that each sound in the English language has a graphic representation.

Blending Auditory skill that increases phonological awareness of the sound structure of words in which phonemes are spoken without pausing between words in order to say a word.

Consonant Phoneme that is not a vowel and is formed with obstruction of the flow of air with the teeth, lips, or tongue.

Consonant Digraph Written letter combination that corresponds to one speech sound but is not represented by one letter alone. Examples: *th, ph, sh, tch.*

Continuous Sound Letter-sound that can be held without distorting the sound. Examples: *a, e, f, i, l, m, n, o, r, s, u, v, w, y, z.*

Digraph Two or three consecutive letters that represent one sound. There are both consonant digraphs and vowel digraphs. Examples: *th, sh, tch, ai, ay, ir, igh, ea, ee, aw.*

Diphthong Complex speech sound that begins with one vowel sound and gradually changes to another vowel sound within the same syllable. Examples: */oi/* in *oil* and */ou/* in *house.*

Grapheme Letter or letter combination that spells a single phoneme. In English a grapheme may be one to four letters, such as *e, ei, igh,* and *eigh.*

Multisyllabic Having more than one syllable.

Phonemic Awareness The awareness of the phonemes that make up spoken words.

Phonics Study of the relationships between letters and the sounds they represent; sound-symbol correspondences. Refers to the system by which symbols represent sounds in an alphabetic writing system.

Phonological Awareness The awareness that oral language consists of words and that words consist of sounds.

Phonology Rule system within a language by which phonemes are sequenced and uttered to make words; study of the unconscious rules that govern speech-sound production.

***r*-controlled** Pertaining to a vowel immediately followed by the consonant *r,* such that its pronunciation is affected, or even dominated, by the */r/* sound.

Schwa Nondistinct vowel found in unstressed syllables in English.

Scope and Sequence *Scope* refers to the amount or range of information contained in the curriculum. *Sequence* is the order in which the information and/or skills are presented.

Segmenting Auditory skill that increases phonological awareness of the sound structure of words in which phonemes within a word are spoken separately, drawing attention to each separate sound. In this curriculum, continuous sounds are held for two or three seconds, and stop sounds are spoken quickly when segmenting to help emphasize each separate sound.

Stop Sound Speech sound that is articulated with a stop of the airstream. The sound cannot be held without distortion. Stop sounds are all consonants (although not all consonants are stop sounds). Examples: *b, c, d, g, h, j, k, p, q, t.*

Syllable Unit of pronunciation that is organized around a vowel. It may or may not have consonants before or after the vowel.

Tricky Words (Sight Words) Words taught as whole words and explained as not following the regular sound-spelling rules.

Unstressed Unaccented syllable within a word.

Voiced Speech sound articulated with vibrating vocal cords.

Vowel Open phoneme that is the nucleus of every syllable. English has eighteen vowel phonemes.